WORDPRESS FOUNDATIONS

BY JASON ANNAS

EnlightenedWebmastery.com

Proudly Present

WORDPRESS FOUNDATIONS

BY JASON ANNAS

A comprehensive up to date workbook on understanding and mastering WordPress.

WordPress Foundations

Presented by:

EnlightenedWebmastery.com

Copyright © 2009 by Jason Annas.

For general information on our other products, please visit our website at **www.enlightenedwebmastery.com.**

Last edited on December 10, 2008

Table of Contents

Chapter 1

Introduction to the book

What is WordPress exactly? WordPress is an open-source blog publishing system that is written in PHP, and is released under the GNU general public license. The program uses MySQL databases to store your information. As of this writing, the latest version is 2.6, which was released on July 15th, 2008.

In today's mobile age, we are constantly on the run. The Internet is a moving medium, constantly changing and evolving. In the past, if you wanted to add some news to your website, or add a "blog" post, you had to go home, open up your HTML editor (notepad, textedit, vi, or if you were lucky DreamWeaver) and type in your content. You would then need to FTP into your server, replace the index / home page with your new page, and update all links as needed on your webpage. If you wanted to make a new category on your site you would need to update the ENTIRE website, you would need to re-upload the newly edited pages to your server. This process is fully manual.

This is how we had to do things back in the day, and is why in not too much time, people started creating content management systems (CMS for short). With these, you could login to a special part of the website, type in some information, and it was automatically updated on your website. You did not need to re-upload pages, or change links. Everything was stored in a special database, and a programming language would call up that data, or any other data required, and dynamically load it onto the website.

I can't begin to tell you how amazing that was, the only downside was, if you didn't know how to program one, you were going to have to pay an expensive price. I learned how to program these using mysql and php, and trust me, back then it was not something you wanted to do.

Fast-forward to today, and you have many different fully automated, and free CMS systems. I have used most everyone available, my favorite being WordPress. For some reason, I always find myself coming back to this platform. With this one tool, you can make a powerful, high end, beautiful looking website, while having complete control over everything on your website, for free.

With *wordpress.com*, you can sign up, and everything is done automatically for you. You get free hosting, a free domain, and you get the WordPress software pre-installed for you. It does NOT get any simpler than this!

Throughout this book, I will be presenting to you the main parts of WordPress. I will be giving you screen shots, step by step tutorials, in a way that you do not need to read from page 1 to end. You will gain the strength, and know how to go out, and build a blog of your own, have it on the Internet, and have users beating down your server to view your content. It's an exiting ride, and I can't wait for us to get started and for you to get your blog online.

Topics Covered in WordPress Foundations

In this book I will take you by the hand, assuming very little, and get you started blogging in the shortest amount of time possible.

You will learn how to setup a freely hosted account at wordpress.com, and use this for your main platform (I will focus mainly on this throughout the book, and have a separate section devoted to self hosting specific features).

- An in-depth look at the Dashboard interface, and talk about the various options so you can get started quickly.

- How to write posts, including some simple ideas on how to come up with things to say.

- Writing pages, and how they differ from posts.

- Adding multimedia such as video from YouTube, an audio file, or images.

- Mastering categories and tags.

- Ways to work with comments that are added to your blog, and what to do about spam.

- How to add users to your blog, such as friends who will post, or family members you want to help post.

- Using themes, what to look for, and how to apply them right away for that unique look.

Chapter 1 - Introduction to the book

- Understanding RSS and what it can do for you.

- Basic tasks you should do to keep your blog up.

- How to get people to view your blog, and enjoy what you write.

- Learn some cool resources that you can get ongoing support, and many other things.

What you need to follow along in this book

I want this book to be as open and easy as can be. Fast clear information. I want this to be used as a guide, and a reference. As such you are NOT required to read this from page 1 to the end. All that is required is you go to the topic of most interest to you.

However, I did design this as a workbook. Some chapters will NOT be for you (such as password protection, adding users, and some of the more advanced stuff I added near the end of the book).

If you are a beginner, I have laid out this course in a manner most conducive to you. If you follow along and do the exercises, you will have a fully functional blog up and running in however long it takes you to get through this guide. (You could just read the summaries, and be up and running in about an hour, and come back and re-read the meaty sections as time goes on to fully grasp the concepts).

When you finish a chapter, you can continue, or play around with what you learned, and come back later on, to further cement the ideas you have learned. All you need to know is covered here to get you started.

As far as technical skills are required, all you need to know is how to check your email, read this book, follow along, be dedicated, and most of all, have fun!

Feedback

Please feel free to send me feedback. I want to know what you think about the Book, the parts you liked, or disliked, how much it helped you, and what you would like to learn in the future. Help me help you.

Free content updates and much more

After you buy this book, please sign up for our newsletter at enlightenedwebmastery.com, and I will send you a free bonus report on how to create and edit graphics using free technology over the web, requiring no installations, and can be done at any computer with Internet access. The members of this list also get fantastic free content, and information on the latest happens, as well as what products we are currently developing. I will be make videos based on your feedback, and give them to you via this newsletter.

Chapter 1 - Introduction to the book

When your are through with this book or course, please go to enlightenedwebmastery.com and use the contact me form and send me a link to your blog, I'm thinking of having a showcase so others can see your blog and you can show it off to the world =).

Also, in case you do not read the book from front to back, if you bought this book from Amazon, you get a special discount on the course, check out the last chapter for more details. It's geared towards taking your blog and your success to a higher level. (And you get instant access to it when you pay).

Talk soon,

Jason

P.S. I am very proud of this workbook and course, I know it will let you accomplish what you want to do SO MUCH FASTER and with LESS HASSLE than I did.

Best of luck on your site, and your success, ok, lets get started...

Chapter 2

Blogging Basics

So what exactly is a "blog" anyway?

A "Blog" is a shortening of the words web and log. For you and me, it is a website for personal or professional use, maintained by one person, that is updated frequently, and is set up in such a way that other people on the internet can read it, and comment on the material.

A blog can contain not only text, but you can have music, video, or photos in addition to your text. Blogs started out being used as journals, and they still are, a place where you can share the goings on of your mind with the world at large.

Please be aware, that blogging is a public medium, and as such, you do not necessarily want to publish your most private thoughts. It's a good idea to not post things you do not want thrown back in your face. Drinking parties, cheating on your loved one, or how you just scammed someone. These can lead to a series of problems. Many people have gotten fired, divorced, or worse, due to what they wrote on their blogs.

What are the different types of blogs out there?

There are many different types of blogs out there. Most of them fall under a few categories. The main ones being as followed:

(1) Typical   (2) Photo   (3) Video

On a typical blog, you will find news posting, mainly text, but many include pictures to make the entries look better. The main point behind this kind of blog is to share stuff with friends as well as the world. They are the normal type of blog you will see on the Internet, they are very easy to maintain, and are quite simple as well.

Photoblogs exist to showcase your photography, or other graphical work, such as 3d renders, 2d drawings, or graphic design artwork you wish to show off. You do not need to be a professional photographer to have a photo blog, but please be aware of the copyrights prior to putting images on your blog. Many people host their images on Flickr, Google's Picasa Web, zoomr, imageshack.us or SmugMug. This benefits you many ways. No bandwidth limitations, and the images are hosted on a secondary source. Meaning if your blog dies, your images are still online for you and the world to see. My personal photography site has the images hosted on flickr so you can view my photos on flickr or my website.

Video blogs are blogs that typically serve video. Many people will post their favorite YouTube movies on their blog to share with the world. I am not a lawyer, but the best I understand, it is ok to embed YouTube videos on your site of anything (provided it is NOT illegal material), if the owner does not want it shared, he can set that option up on his account.

Many people upload videos to YouTube, just to post them on their blog. If you are using wordpress.com to host your blog, you will need to do this as well, because you cannot upload videos to your account. Plus when you use YouTube, it uses YouTube's bandwidth, opposed to yours. Thus allowing you to keep your costs down. You can check out a site I made as an example for this book called – *TheTVReview.com*, you will be greeted to a photo, and when you click that photo it opens up a video that is hosted on YouTube.

Blogging Terminology

If you are going to be a blogger, you must know a few common terms, else you will be pulling your hair out with frustration.

At the heart of any blog are its posts. When you write something on your blog, that is a post. When you post something on your blog, WordPress creates something called a **permalink**, which is a fancy term for a permanent link to your post. You can give this URL how to anyone to view that specific post.

When you write a post, (provided you have **comments** enabled), someone can **comment** on your blog. What this means is underneath your post, you will see a comments section. Random people on the Internet will be able to post a comment on your post. It is up to you if you want this functionality on your blog or not. Some do, some do not. Most successful blogs have comments enabled. This is a great way to form a community, and encourages people to return to your site. With WordPress, you can disable the ability to comment on a post-by-post basis.

Another term you may not be familiar with is called **Trackbacks**. What a trackback is essentially, is when you post a new article on your website, and someone views that post and makes a comment on their blog about your post, it will automatically display a trackback under your comments section. This will show up as a link under your comments and will look something like this. [...] various text here [...] those "..." mean there is something before or after this comment. You should be aware that spammers abuse this system to advertise on your blog. So you may want to keep checking on your comments so you can stop this if you are getting spammed.

Another recent term is **RSS**. What RSS does is allow someone to subscribe to your site, and read your material from their RSS reader, opposed to visiting your website. This can be both good, and bad. I personally use an RSS feeder, and have some blogs set up there, as I like to be notified of updates on sites I really enjoy. If you sign up with feedburner, you can set it up so users can subscribe to your feed, and get email updates when you post a new article.

Chapter 3

Choosing which version of WordPress to use

The Different WordPress Services

WordPress offers four different "classes" of service. The first three are free; the fourth is for large companies who need support. That version will not be covered in this book.

WordPress.com - This is the version we will be covering in exhaustive detail. This version is hosted at wordpress.com, as such; you do not need to pay anything. It is a free turnkey solution. You go to *wordpress.com*, create an account and your running (I will show you how to do this soon).

Wordpress.org - This version will be covered here as well, but not extensively, as the individual parts that make this so different could cover multiple books. With this version you need 2 things: A host (one that supports WordPress, PHP and MySQL) this usually costs money, and a domain name. An example name is *you.com.*

WordPress MU - You get this at *http://mu.wordpress.org* The benefit of using this is it allows you to create a network of blogs all housed under a single domain name. This is not meant for individual users; rather, it is intended for large corporations, which have multiple blogs (thousands even) on the same domain, using the same server. We will not be covering this version of WordPress, as it is not something most people will use.

WordPress KWEE - This is the Enterprise edition, known as the "KnowNow WordPress Enterprise Edition." It is only available for Fortune 500 companies. It competes with other enterprise class platforms, and thus not for you or me. We will also not be covering this version.

What are the major differences?

In this book, we are focusing mainly on wordpress.com. Wordpress.com is a self-hosted service. It's like your email account. You do not pay for the name (Gmail, yahoo, hotmail, etc), you do not pay for the hosting (unless your using a premium account, and even then your not administering the host), you just get to use the service, and enjoy all that it entails.

The benefits to this are many. For self-hosting you will need a domain which costs about 10$, and hosting which will cost a similar amount or more. Hosting is a monthly fee, so you will need to pay for this each month. To start using the self-hosted version, you will need to upload WordPress to your server, create a database, a username, and install WordPress and set it up. So besides saving money, you also save time and a lot of hassle. Not many people want to deal with all this work for a personal blog. This is why we are mainly focused on wordpress.com. I highly recommend it, if for no other reason than to see how you like it, before your rush out and spend some money on hosting.

I recommend HostGator, Dreamhost, and Imountain for hosting. These are places I have used in the past with great success. Imountain is a "green" hosting company, and I use them currently.

The benefits of using Self-Hosting over the free wordpress.com are many.

- No advertising.

- Complete Control.

- You can upload videos.

- You can download free plugins and widgets.

- You can download custom themes, and make your own to get your own distinct look.

- And many more which will be brought to light later on.

Now to look at the bad:

- You have to have your own server

- You need your own domain name

- You have to install it

- You have to keep it up to date, and upgrade it on your own.

- And a few more things.

I think the benefits FAR outweigh the cons, but if you are starting out, it makes sense to use the free version first.

With that said, many people use the self-hosted version, because you have much more flexibility in what you can do and use. The beauty is, the dashboard and usability between the self-hosted (wordpress.org) and the free hosted (wordpress.com) are the same, if you know one, you know the other. There are a few slight differences in how you use things, but we will cover those as we get to them.

You are not wasting your time learning wordpress.com, so please do not think so, what you are doing is getting used to using the interface, so you have a good idea of how you like the platform, and get comfortable using it, and maybe drawing in some traffic or business, prior to spending money and time on the self-hosted version (which I cover how to set-up near the end of the book).

Chapter 4

Getting started with WordPress.com

Creating an account

To create an account, follow along with me, as I set up an account. Please remember you need to come up with your own user name. The name you want to use may not be available, if you are really stuck on using that name, something you can do is add numbers to the end, such as wordpress76.

Please note your username will be the same name as your hosted domain. The URL for your blog will be username.wordpress.com. So please take notice before you start your blog. Ilikepinkbunnies may be a good username, but if your blog has to deal with cooking, well.... that might be bad...

First off, go to *http://www.wordpress.com* and click the big button that says "Sign Up Now!".

Now you need to come up with a username, remember what I wrote previously and choose accordingly.

You will need to give a real email address, so make note of that, and you need to have some numbers in your password. Please do not just write your user name or email as the password, as it will be very easy to guess, and someone may steal your account.

When you are finished, click Next ->.

On this screen you are given the option to change your domain name, so it is different than your user name, and give your blog a title.

The language option is the language you will be typing in, if your typing will be in Spanish choose Spanish, otherwise leave it as English. This will not affect your menu items; you change that in a different section in the dashboard, which we will go over soon.

Your next choice is the following: "I would like my blog to appear in search engines like Google and Technorati, and in public listings around WordPress.com."

For almost EVERYTHING you do, you want this box checked, so others can find your website. As this is a test website, I am not clicking this button, but in real life, this is a button you would click.

When you are finished click the Signup button and continue on to the next page.

Type in your first name, and last name, as well as some detail about yourself. When you are finished click "save profile".

Check your email, you should see an email from WordPress; you need to open that email and click the link.

How to Log Into Your WordPress.com Account

Now that your account is ready, you can login to your blog, and take a look around the dashboard.

Please take note of this link, and post it in your bookmarks, as it will allow you instant access to your blog.

username.wordpress.com/wp-login.php

You need to replace username your account name (or domain name) on the previous screens. Self-hosted is u.com/wp-login.php

In my example, I would type in

wpfoundations for the username,

with *test1234* as password

Please note, if you click remember me, a cookie will get placed inside your browser, and whenever you visit this site with the same browser it will remember you. In other words, you do not want to do this on a public machine, or someone else's computer. The same thing applies when your browser asks if you want it to remember your password.

This is perfectly fine on your home machine though.

You are now logged into your blog. This is the dashboard. This is the gateway into your blog.

This is where you will manage your blog.

To log out of your blog at any time, click the Log Out option at the top.

By default, when you create your blog, WordPress will apply a theme, throw in some widgets, and include a post on your blog. The blog title you gave earlier on will show up on the header graphic on your site.

To visit your site, while you are in dashboard, click the visit my site link, or type in *username.wordpress.com.*

http://wpfoundations.wordpress.com/

You can see the sample post, on the left. On the far right, you see a "sidebar", in it you have a search widget at the top, links to your "Pages", an Archives widget, Categories widget, Blog roll "links" widget, and the Meta widget, which allows you to do some administrative work on your site.

This is completely customizable, and we will get into how to edit it all later on in the book.

Chapter 5

Getting started with Dashboard

New in 2.7

WordPress 2.7 has a new revamped dashboard interface. This can be both exciting and terrifying. The point behind the new interface was to avoid having to load up new screens just to access a certain menu. The goal was to have the most used parts accessible within 1-2 clicks.

Some of the other cool new features are, you can change how your dashboard looks when you login. You can move your panels around "modules" such as you can have **stats** at the top right, **right now** (at a glance which lets you see if you got any new comments, how many posts you have, etc) on the left. It's pretty nice, if there is a feature you keep using, now you can keep it near the top so you can always access it. (please note, if your using .org you will need to install the WordPress stats plug-in to be able to use that module)

Another great feature is you can click "New Post" from the contextual menu located at the top.

QuickPress is a new feature that lets you start up a post right from your dashboard. You can give your post a title or write the body text, add images or movies and tags (no categories). You can click save draft, and come back and work on it later, or click "Publish" and it will be live on your site right away.

Recent Comments lets you not only see the most recent comments, but it also lets you moderate them directly from the dashboard module. Which is a very welcome and helpful feature.

Understanding the Interface

Here is a picture of what the main interface looks like:

Clicking the title and dragging it around can move the larger "modules", or you can minimize it by clicking the far right corner (an arrow will show up when you hover over it). You can also turn them off by using the screen options menu at the top.

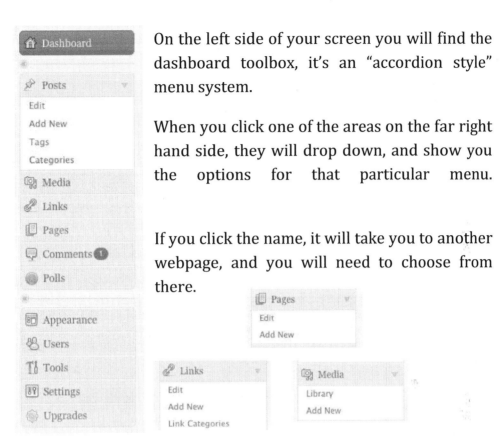

On the left side of your screen you will find the dashboard toolbox, it's an "accordion style" menu system.

When you click one of the areas on the far right hand side, they will drop down, and show you the options for that particular menu.

If you click the name, it will take you to another webpage, and you will need to choose from there.

Posts – This is the menu that allows you to choose to write a new post (Add New), manage your tags, manage your categories, or edit an already existing post. When you click "Posts" your taken to the same menu as if you clicked edit.

Media – This is the menu that allows you to manage your media library, or go ahead and upload a new file to your blog.

Links – This lets you add new links to your blog roll, edit already existing ones, or create categories for them. (i.e. friends, stores)

Pages – This lets you either edit or create a new page from scratch.

Comments – This tells you if you have any comments that need to be approved (notice the bright red 1), this menu does not drop down, but takes you right to the edit comments module (which you also can access on your main dashboard).

The next pane varies depending on if your using wordpress.com or wordpress.org. I will discuss the differences.

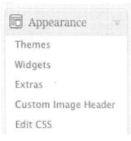

The difference between them are, the .org allows you to use plugins, and the wordpress.com lets you upgrade your account to have more space, and be able to edit css.

WordPress.com lets you use the custom image header (chapter 12) to personalize your blog. Extras are for allowing snapshots, and more (read the extras chapter for more).

Themes – By choosing themes you can change your theme on the fly. (WordPress.org shows Theme Editor, where you can edit the individual php pages, and css code).

Widgets – These add additional functionality to your blog (search, calendar, and more)

Edit CSS - is for WordPress.com users, it allows you to modify your css, and see how it will look. If you want to use this feature you need to pay some extra cash (check the extras chapter).

If you are using a custom theme, or one you made yourself with extra functions, you may see additional options on your menu that lets you adjust theme specific features (such as special sliders)

Users - let you Add new users to your account, and manage who is there.

Tools – this is a new feature that I'm not going into here. But basically it lets you install "gears" (gears.google.com) which let's you speed up how pages load, and enable new features.

Settings – this is where you can adjust various settings for your blog, we will be covering this later.

Plugins (.org only) this lets you see which ones you have installed, let you activate new ones, edit them, or see custom plug-ins that have special options that you need to manage.

A Few New Modules

I'm going to show you the new Right Now module, Recent Comments, Recent Drafts, and the QuickPress here. These are available on both .com and .org

Right Now

At a Glance

6	Posts	4	Comments
3	Pages	2	Approved
4	Categories	1	Pending
14	Tags	1	Spam

Theme ChaoticSoul with 5 Widgets   Change Theme

Akismet has protected your site from 1 spam comment already, and there's 1 comment in your spam queue right now.

Right Now - this is a fun new module. You can see at a glance your posts, how many comments you have, how many need approval, and more. This menu is also color-coded. Bad things are Red, stuff that is pending is Yellow, and good things are Green.

QuickPress

Title My New Catchy Title!

Upload/Insert

Content Showcasing WordPress's snazzy new QuickPress feature!

Tags fun, wordpress, quickpress,

Save Draft   Cancel   Publish

QuickPress – From here you can write a new post. You can also save that post as a draft and access it using the new Recent Drafts module.

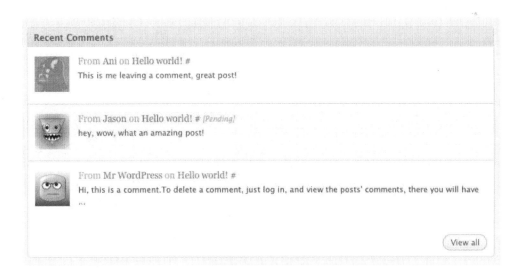

Recent Drafts – This lets you see the latest drafts you have wrote, and be able to change them by clicking on them.

Recent Comments – from this interface, you can hover over each comment and approve, unapproved and more. This is a very useful feature and a huge timesaver.

Chapter 5 - Getting started with Dashboard

Chapter 6

Setting up your blog

Editing Your Profile

Before we get started making content, we need to set some options on your user profile, and perform some tasks.

The quickest way to get there, is to click your name at the top of the dashboard, you will then see the following:

Editing Your Profile and Personal Options

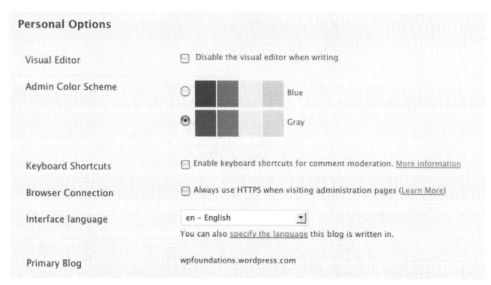

The visual editor allows you instant access to high end formatting options, such as bolding, setting header information, as well as allowing other various formatting options, right from the interface itself. I highly recommend keeping this box checked.

The color scheme is a preference for you to choose, I'm keeping mine as gray.

The interface language is what the interface language is, this is not what your content will be wrote in, just the interface. If you are not a native speaker, you might want to change the option to your language of choice to better navigate the interface with ease.

Primary Blog is the link to your main blog on wordpress.com, if you have another blog on wordpress.com you can change whichever you want to be your Primary.

To the right of this screen, you get the option of uploading your picture. This can be you, or an "avatar" image. Click Choose File, and select one from your hard drive, then click Upload Image.

Your image needs to be around 128x128, so after you upload this image, you will need to "crop the image" which means making it fit into those boundaries.

You will be whisked away to a screen similar to this:

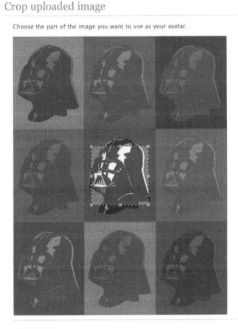

The square with "marching ants" is your 128x128 boundary. If you want to resize, only click on the corner boundaries, as I did here.

When you are happy with your selection, click crop, and you will be taken to the next page.

Your new avatar will show up now, both on your blog, and on wordpress.com.

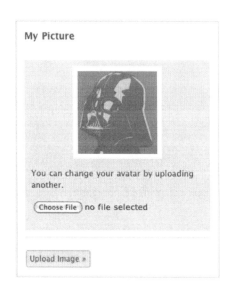

All done!

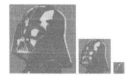

Your avatar image has been uploaded and you should start seeing it appear around WordPress.com soon!

Updating Your Name and Personal Details

Name

Username	wpfoundations	Your username cannot be changed
First name	Anakin	
Last name	Skywalker	
Nickname	Ani	
Display name publicly as	wpfoundations ⬍	

You cannot change your username. Input a First name, and a Last name. Then proceed with a Nickname.

Whenever you hit "Update" at the bottom, you will then be able to change your online name via a drop down box.

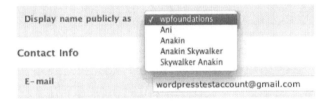

If you wish to change your main email at any point, please do so here. Insert any website you wish to be displayed under your profile here (you can list a website other than the wordpress.com url, as I did here).

AIM is your AOL instant messenger nick, same with yahoo, and Google. These are entirely optional.

Contact Info

E-mail	wordpresstestaccount@gmail.com	Required
Website	wordpressfoundations.com	
AIM		
Yahoo IM		
Jabber / Google Talk		

Now you can insert some information about you and your hobbies.

About Yourself

| Biographical Info | When I'm not running The Galactic Empire, I like to blog about my evil doings on wordpress.com. |
| | Share a little biographical information to fill out your profile. This may be shown publicly. |

After that, we need to change your password, to something more secure. Try adding numbers, uppercase letters, and symbols. You need to remember this, so don't make it hard on yourself, you just don't want people stealing your account. A good example password is - w0rdPre$$.

When you are done, click the Update Profile button below, and then click "Settings" at the top.

When you are done, click the Update Profile button below, then click the settings tab on the left, and choose "General".

Now we need to work on updating the settings on the blog, and making it more personal for us.

Configuring The Settings For Your Blog.

General Settings

Blog Title	WordPress Foundations – The official unofficial blc
Tagline	Become a WordPress Jedi overnight with wordpres *In a few words, explain what this blog is about.*
Language	en – English ▾
	Language this blog is primarily written in.
	You can also modify the interface language in your profile.
E-mail address	wordpresstestaccount@gmail.com
	This address is used only for admin purposes. If you change this we will send you an email at your new address to confirm it. **The new address will not become active until confirmed.**
Timezone	UTC –4 ▾ hours *UTC time is 2008-12-08 1:13:11* *UTC –4 is 2008-12-07 21:13:11*
	Unfortunately, you have to manually update this for Daylight Savings Time. Lame, we know, but will be fixed in the future.
Date Format	● December 7, 2008
	○ 2008/12/07
	○ 12/07/2008
	○ 07/12/2008
	○ Custom: F j, Y December 7, 2008
	Documentation on date formatting. Click "Save Changes" to update sample output.
Time Format	● 9:13 pm
	○ 9:13 PM
	○ 21:13
	○ Custom: g:i a 9:13 pm
Week Starts On	Sunday ▾

Save Changes

The Blog Title will appear on the "Header" of your blog, which is located at the top.

The Tagline is what is listed below your Header.

Language tells wordpress.com what language you are writing in.

Email is your current email address.

Membership, is if you want people to create accounts on your website before they can comment, its up to you if you want to do this or not. I don't because when I go to someone's blog, and I have to sign up, I just won't comment.

Time zone. Look at the UTC time, see what it is, and the difference between UTC and your time. Then select that option.

You can change the **Date and Time format** if you want; I like this default setting, as it works for us in the US.

Here you can choose what day of the week is the start for you. In the US it is Sunday. The default is Monday.

Be sure to hit the **"Save Changes"** button at the bottom.

Then click on the "writing" option under Settings on the left (under General).

Changing The Writing and Reading Settings on Your Blog.

Writing Settings

Size of the post box	20 lines
Formatting	☑ Convert emoticons like :-) and :-P to graphics on display ☐ WordPress should correct invalidly nested XHTML automatically
Default Post Category	Random ⬍
Default Link Category	Blogroll ⬍

Size of the post box - how big your editor box is.

Formatting - changes smiles into graphical smiles.

Default Post Category - the default category for your posts. If you write mainly news, choose news.

Default Link Category - Change your default Link categories.

Save Changes, and Click Reading.

Reading Settings

Front page displays	◉ Your latest posts
	○ A static page (select below)
	   • Front page: [– Select – ▾]
	   • Posts page: [– Select – ▾]

Blog pages show at most	[10] posts
Syndication feeds show the most recent	[10] posts
For each article in a feed, show	◉ Full text ○ Summary
For each article in an enhanced feed, show	☐ Categories ☑ Tags ☑ Comment count ☐ Add to Stumbleupon ☑ Add to Del.icio.us ☑ Add to Digg.com ☐ Add to Reddit Changes may not appear until you create a new post or your news reader refreshes.
Encoding for pages and feeds	[UTF-8] The character encoding you write your blog in (UTF-8 is recommended)

<u>Front-page displays</u> - choose if you want a certain post to always be on your home page.

<u>Blog pages show at most</u> - How many pages to show at most. When you have more, it will show a previous or next.

<u>Syndication feeds show the most recent</u> - How many feeds show up when someone subscribes to your RSS Feed (I bump this to 12-15 normally).

<u>For each article in a feed, show</u> - If you want people who subscribe via RSS to get the full post, or just a summary.

<u>For each article in an enhanced feed, show</u> - For those readers, what do you want to show up in your feed.

<u>Encoding for pages and feeds</u> - Leave the encoding alone, it is what you need, unless you need something else, and if you do, you will know.

Click "Save Changes"

Setting the Discussion Options for your Blog

Discussion Settings

Default article settings	☑ Attempt to notify any blogs linked to from the article (slows down posting.)
	☑ Allow link notifications from other blogs (pingbacks and trackbacks.)
	☑ Allow people to post comments on the article
	(These settings may be overridden for individual articles.)

The first options means while you are posting something to your blog, and commenting about another blog, it will automatically put a pingback to that article on the other person's blog.

The second option is whenever someone else writes a post about something you posted and links to it, they will ping back your article, and it will appear under the comments on your blog.

The last option is if you want to allow others the ability to leave comments on the article. I highly recommend this, as I see no point in having a blog without comments.

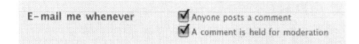

You can have WordPress automatically email you whenever someone makes a post on your blog, or when a comment is being held for moderation.

If you check the first option, you will have to approve every post. If you are really worried about spam, this can be a great idea to have checked. You will need to check your comments constantly to keep approving them, and this can become real tedious if your site becomes popular.

The second option means when someone posts, they have to enter their name and email.

Third means if you set it up so you have to approve everything, if this user has already been approved, he can go ahead and post without needing clearance.

Comment Moderation

Hold a comment in the queue if it contains a certain number or more links. (A common characteristic of comment spam is a large number of hyperlinks.) This can be a good way to stop spam, I keep it at 2, which is fine for the most part, because someone might be replying to my post and posting a link to help. Some people really do post valid links, sometimes multiple links; it pays to check your comments, as you could be getting real posts that are not spam.

When a comment contains any of these words in its content, name, URL, e-mail, or IP, it will be held in the moderation queue. One word or IP per line. It will match inside words, so "press" will match "WordPress".

If you don't want certain topics being posted, you can fix it so these kinds of posts do not show up. Such as "Religion", "Politics", "Sex" or anything else you do not want talked about in the comments of your blog.

If you put the words as Backlist, the comment will automatically be marked as spam, and you have a chance to review it, but in 15 days it is GONE.

Enabling Avatars on Your Blog

An avatar is an image-based representation of you. We set up one earlier when we setup the profile for this account. People associate you with your avatar, if you use the same one on multiple forums; it helps people keep track of you. If you used my avatar I setup here for an example, people would remember you as the pink Vader, regardless of your nick.

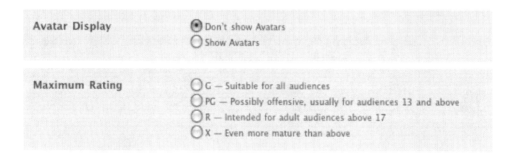

You have the option of allowing this or not. I would, as they are fun to look at, and add personality.

You can setup a rating, so inappropriate avatars do not show up on your site.

If your running your local church's website, you do not want people commenting with naked people or curse words on their images. I think PG is a good setting to choose, it's not too restrictive.

The next thing you can do, is choose a default Avatar.

The first is the "Mystery Man" which you cannot see here, but is just a gray picture of a man.

Blank is Blank.

Gravatar is the logo for that company.

The next 3 are randomly generated, each user will have a different avatar, and will be unique to them, and thus, not inappropriate in the least.

Click "save" and move on to Privacy Settings.

Adjusting The Privacy Settings of Your Blog.

Privacy Settings

Blog Visibility
- I would like my blog to be visible to everyone, including search engines (like Google, Sphere, Technorati) and archivers
- I would like to block search engines, but allow normal visitors
- I would like my blog to be visible only to users I choose

Blog Visibility
- I would like my blog to be visible to everyone, including search eng
- I would like to block search engines, but allow normal visitors
- I would like my blog to be visible only to users I choose

Up to 35 users allowed to access blog. Want more?

Username: [   ]   Add User

(1) I would like my blog to be visible to everyone, including search engines (like Google, Sphere, and Technorati) and archive's.

This is the option you need to select if you want your blog indexed (and you usually do)

(2) I would like to block search engines, but allow normal visitors.

This means anyone can visit your blog, they just need to know the address.

(3) I would like my blog to be visible only to users I choose.

This means you need to send out invites, and the user needs to have a wordpress.com account. You can only have 35 users, so choose this option quite wisely.

Click Save Changes.

Delete Blog, deletes your blog! Media lets you choose the dimensions of the images that are displayed on your blog. OpenID is a special feature that let's you login to OpenID based sites using your login here. Domains, is a paid feature. It costs 10 dollars per year. It allows you.com to point to you.wordpress.com.

Chapter 6 - Setting up your blog

Chapter 7

Writing Posts

Accessing the Writing Panel

At the top of your wordpress.com dashboard (top right), click "new post" and you will see something similar to the following.

Writing Your First Post

While you are in this panel, we may as well go over how to write a post on your blog. This is where you will be spending most of your time in dashboard, so lets go over how. I will discuss this from the top down. Starting with the Title, which is what you see at top.

1 - You put the **title** here (at the top), this is what will be part of your permalink, and will show up in search engines and throughout your blog.

2 - This is the **menu bar**, if you click the last button, it opens up everything, including the kitchen sink. This is where you select if you want to bold items, make lists, create quotes, or spell check.

3 - This is where you **write** your post.

4 – This is where you write an **excerpt**. This is very important as it keeps you from adding duplicate content to your site.

5 – Send **Trackbacks** is for if you want to send trackbacks.

6 – **Discussion** is where you choose if you want to enable comments or not.

On the right hand panel from top to bottom

1 – **Publish** - this will publish your post for the world to see.

2 - Create some **tags**. This is a newer feature of WordPress; I find it essential in my everyday use. When you click on a tag, it will bring up similar posts to that tag, all dynamically. You can also display a visual cloud on your blog, and the popular tags are largest.

3 - You need to create a **category** or select one that you have already made, to keep your posts organized.

Here is what your page might look like after you type in some content:

I created a post with a list and a quote, and added in some tags along with a category.

We have a problem here, check out the link below.

Permalink: http://wpfoundations.wordpress.com/2008/07/22/a-catchy-title...-my-first-post/ Edit

This is not the kind of link you want on your blog. It is far to long, and not appropriate for our needs. You need to change it. Click the edit button, and change it to something shorter as below.

Permalink: http://wpfoundations.wordpress.com/2008/07/22/catchy-first-post/ Edit

This is a much simpler URL, and will be easier to remember. Please check this before you publish any article to ensure that you have a URL that you like.

The fine art of tagging

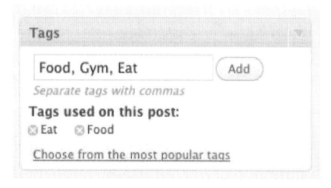

When you create tags, you need to try and stay consistent.

Let's say you're writing a video-gaming blog, and in particular you're writing about Grand Theft Auto IV. Lets say you wrote an article about the game, and tagged it GTA4. Next week comes, you wrote some more articles, wasn't sure what you tagged the last GTA release as, and decide to tag it GTA IV. When you, or someone else, clicks GTA IV, they will not see the content tagged as GTA4, only the content with the tag GTA IV. This is a common mistake people make when creating tags, this is common because you can write hundreds of different tags, and you have no way of seeing what you previous wrote when you are writing tags for your new post.

Tags are very powerful, I just want you to try and be consistent with your labeling, to avoid you and your readers some frustration. When someone gets to your site via a Google search, they see the tag, and when they click it, they either will, or will not see the related content, depending on if you tagged it right.

Categories

It is a good practice to keep your categories to a minimum, and use tags to their full advantage. This way you can keep your categories very focused. In the previous exampled I talked about a video game. If you had a video game blog and made a category for every game that came out, you would soon have far to many categories to manage or to be of any real use.

A better plan would be as follows. Xbox 360, PS3, and Wii. Opposed to making categories for each game. This way you can make a new post for one game, and categorize it per system, and tag the post for that game. When a user comes to your site via Google, they can click on that tag to read more on that game, or the category to read about more games for that platform. This example works regardless if you are doing a blog on games or not. You can categorize music, news, movies, etc. I highly recommend keeping your categories to a minimum, and use tags as much as possible.

If you checkout the example site I setup during the making of this book, *TheTVReview.com* you will see that I use categories for the names of TV shows, I'm using tags (though the public cannot see them), for each show, a set of tags might be, HBO, 5 Stars, DVD, Review, The Wire. These are internal right now, I will be forming a tag cloud, and so you can click on those tags to see similar content.

Let's go over the different formatting options available while using the visual editor.

Starting from the top left, lets discuss each of these in detail:

B - This Bolds your text.
I - This provides italics.
ABC - is the strike through option, so you can write ~~stupid~~ smart text and write over it.

The next two buttons create lists, the first one uses bullets, and the second creates numbered lists.

The next button creates a block quote, which is useful when you are quoting and want things to stand out.

The next three buttons determine the alignment of your text, if you want it left aligned, centered, or right aligned.

The next option deals with creating hyper links (these are words you can click and get sent to another website).

 The first button creates a link, to do this, highlight the text you wish to make a link and click that button.

Type in the URL, including http://

The target is if you want the link to open up in a new window or the same window.

Title is what will appear when someone hovers over your link

Class is not something you need to worry about,

Insert/edit link   **X**

Insert/edit link

Link URL	http://www.wordpressfoundations.com
Target	-- Not set --
Title	The comprehensive introduction to wordpre
Class	-- Not set --

Cancel   Insert

The next button inserts a more tag, which lets you write an introductory paragraph, and have only that show up on your front page, it will create a "click here to read more" message, and when they click, they will see the whole post (on a new page).

The next button is your spellchecker. Which helps you check your words for spelling errors.

The next button makes this screen take up your full screen, thus giving you more space to write with.

The last button either shows or hides the kitchen sink.

These are the buttons you see when you show the kitchen sink.

The format drop down menu, lets you select some text, and change how it is formatted. You can make text be a certain style such as a header, or paragraph, etc. This is very useful, and you can change things depending on your theme to get different results.

The next option underlines your text, please be careful with this, as when most people see underlined text they think it is a link.

The next button aligns your text into "full" or justified.

The A will change the color of your text, again be careful with this, as most links are a different color, and this is how some people see links.

The next 2 buttons are for pasting in text from other programs. The first one is from a plain text editor, and the second is for Microsoft Word. It gets rid of all the non-standard junky editing Word applies to the text.

The Eraser will get rid of custom formatting.

The Omega symbol allows you to insert symbols into your blog.

The next two are you undo, and redo's, (does the same thing as cmd z or cntrl z does in your normal programs) allowing you to undo some changes you just made.

The last button is the help button, click it when you need some help.

Learn and Master The Visual Editors Shortcuts

If you want to learn the shortcuts and take full advantage of the rich visual text editor, these shortcuts can save you some time. If your using a Macintosh use **Command + Letter**, if you are running Linux, or Windows, use **Ctrl + letter**.

Action	Letter
Copy	c
Paste	v
Select all	a
Cut	x
Undo	z
Redo	y

These shortcuts require using Alt (option) + Shift + letter.

Action	Letter
Bold	b

Chapter 7 - Writing Posts

Italic	i
Check Spelling	n
Align Left	l
Justify Text	j
Align Center	c
~~Strikethrough~~	d
Align Right	r
List	u
Insert link	a
1. List	o
Remove link	s
Quote	q
Insert Image	m
Full Screen	g
Insert More Tag	t
Insert Page Break tag	p
Help	h
Switch to HTML mode	e

The HTML Editor

If you are a code monkey, who has been writing html since it came out, you may feel more at home writing in this editor, if so, all you need to do is click the "HTML" button at the top, and boom, you are there.

The editor comes with buttons you can press to insert code that works with WordPress. Most people rarely add HTML to a post, and tend to stick with using the Visual Editor. The main reason I use HTML on a WordPress blog, is to add in code, and functionality.

TheTVReview.com (an example site I setup for this book), I write completely in HTML mode. I have special code for the special effects I write, and other special enhanced features that are prevalent on that blog.

But if your not wanting such functionality on your blog, there is no need to ever visit the HTML view, except for quick visits.

I have noticed a bug that whenever I'm in HTML mode, and have some <SCRIPT> code, or <IFRAME> code it disappears when I go back and forth from visual to HTML, so please save often, and copy (CTRL + A or CMD + A) your HTML post before you switch back to visual (if your going between them) to avoid heartache incase something gets deleted.

Chapter 7 - Writing Posts

Publishing Your Post

Now that you have a post ready, and you know the basics of the editor, the next major step for you to do is click publish (at the top right of your post, near the title). This will publish your blog.

When you do this, make sure you click "Visit Site" at the top of your dashboard to see how it looks!

Viewing Your First Post

The new post is posted at the top of the page. Every time you make a post, it is filed in reverse-chronological order. Meaning the newest is at the top.

You can see the date and time this was posted, as well as who wrote it.

You see the tags below the post, clicking on those will take you to similar posts on your blog.

Below that you see the category.

On the right side of your site, (your sidebar) you will see Random as a category, and a 1 by it, this is because we created this category for this post, to visit that post, and any other post filed under that category go to *username.wordpress.com/category/random/* to see all of those posts.

You now know how to create posts, and have an understanding of the dashboard interface; it's time to go over how to create pages.

Chapter 8

Creating pages

How pages differ from posts.

Pages are not typically frequently updated, an exception to that would be if you ran a restaurant and wanted to showcase specials. Since this is important to your site, you need to create a dedicated page for this material. When you have this page, you can give it to anyone, they can then visit your website, view that page and see the specials. Since you will not be showing off older specials, you can change it anytime, and no one will ever see the older content.

Pages are more static compared to your "main content" and as such; you will not be updating pages as often, so it's a good idea to not allow people to be able to comment on these pages. We will go over how to do that shortly. Some other good uses for a Page are an "About Us" or a "Contact Us" form.

Writing Your First Page

On your dashboard, click on the Pages menu on the left hand side, and click "Add New".

This layout is very similar as when you are writing a post, there are some exceptions, Give the page a Title "About Us" and type in some sample information you would want people to see when clicking on the "About Us" page on your blog.

About Us

Permalink: http://wpfoundations.wordpress.com/about-us/ (Edit)

Upload/Insert   Visual HTML

B *I* ABC

Format

We created this course to give users a proper foundational level of knowledge on learning how to use, and understand wordpress. We think these are the pure essentials anyone must know in order to go forward in using wordpress. There is always more to learn, but with this in your hands, you can accomplish most any task that is laid out before you.

Path:

Word count: 63   Last edited by Ani on July 24, 2008 at 12:49 am

Discussion

☐ Allow Comments

☐ Allow Pings

These settings apply to this page only. "Pings" are trackbacks and pingbacks.

I highly recommend deselecting <u>Allow Comments</u>, and <u>Allow Pings</u>, which you will find under the discussions section, then click update.

Now that you have your page written, and those two options deselected, click <u>Publish</u> (same location as before) then click <u>Visit Site</u>, to view your page.

Pages
» About
» About Us

You will see the new Page you just made, we just made <u>About Us</u>, go ahead and click it.

The URL for that page and others you make will be similar to the following - *http://wpfoundations.wordpress.com/about-us/.*

Next we need to cover another task, which is dependent on your theme. Go ahead and make a new Page. Follow along.

We will be using a feature called "Templates" so create a new page, and give it the name, "View our Archives".

Leave the Page blank, as you do not need to type anything.

In the Attributes Panel off to the right, change the template, to archives. When you are through click Publish.

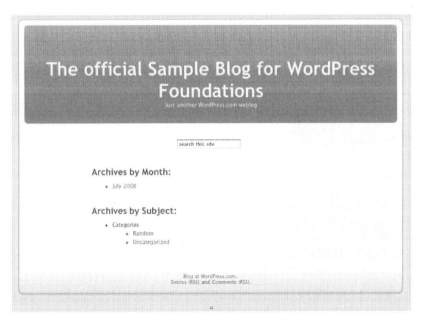

If you do not see this option, it is because your "theme" does not support this template. I'm using the theme that is active when you first get your account to create use this feature.

What this did, was allow WordPress to dynamically create a page for us, that links to the archives on our site. This is a wonderful feature, and some themes offer more or less "Page Templates".

This is why I warned you, if you change to another theme (which we will cover in the next chapter) for your site, you might end up with a blank Page if this "template" is not supported by your "theme".

Chapter 8 - Creating pages

Chapter 9

Applying a theme

How To Choose And Apply a Theme For Your WordPress.com Blog

The default theme of WordPress, is beautiful as is. But some people enjoy having something "custom" or "special", or just need more functionality. In this chapter I will show you 5 of my favorite wordpress.com themes, and show you how to apply them, what to look for, and at the end of the chapter, how to further customize your theme.

If you are using the WordPress.org self-hosted solution, check out the chapter that deals with customizing your blog with wordpress.org. You can still read these parts, as they still apply.

Go to your dashboard, and click open the "Appearance" tab and choose "Themes" and you will see the available themes.

Themes   Widgets   Extras   Custom Image Header   Color Header   Edit CSS

Current Theme

Kubrick by Michael Heilemann
The default WordPress theme complete with customizable header and widgets.

OPTIONS: Widgets | Extras | Custom Image Header | Color Header | Edit CSS

Tags: two columns, fixed width, custom header, blue

Chapter 9 - Applying a theme

Kubrick is the default theme for WordPress. It is a great theme, and may be all you need. If you scroll down below you will see (as of this writing) 5 pages full of themes. Go ahead and click on the name of the one displayed below.

"Ambiru."

Ambiru

A calm, relaxing theme one-column theme with a customizable header.

Tags: one column, custom header, green, custom colors, bottom widgets, fixed width

When you click on it, you will see a preview of how your blog will look if you apply this theme. Go ahead and click the "activate" option on the top right, you can always go back to Kubrick or any other when you want to.

This is now your new theme. Go ahead and click "<u>visit this site</u>" to take a quick peek (I'll wait).

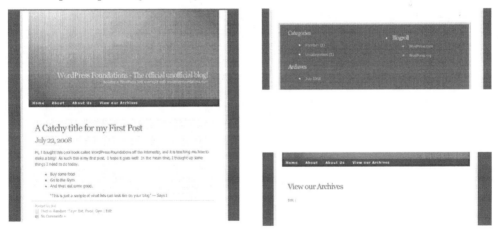

As you can see, your title is posted up top in the header, and your tag line is right below it.

The links to your pages are in the dark gray area (opposed to a sidebar).   And you will also notice, your sidebar, and search function are no longer here.

If you look at the bottom you will see where your blog roll, and links to your archives are now placed.

Remember in the last chapter when we talked about pages, and how you need to be careful when you choose a "Page Template" as not all themes support it?

Go ahead and click View our Archives at the top.

As you can see, it is now "mysteriously" empty. Don't worry, when you switch back to Kubrick or any other theme that supports this "template" it will come back.   That is why you need to be real careful when you change "themes" and take note if it breaks something. Then you will have to decide what is more important to you, that page, or the theme.

Lets go back and lets choose another really good theme.

Likely my favorite wordpress.com theme is, ChaoticSoul by Bryan Veloso. Click it and hit activate.

Current Theme

ChaoticSoul by Bryan Veloso

A dark 2 column theme based off of a certain designer's old website.

OPTIONS: Widgets | Extras | Custom Image Header | Edit CSS

Tags: dark, two columns, black, custom header, fixed width

You will notice, we have search functionality again, the design looks much cleaner, and we have access to our pages, archives, and categories on the far right.

If you click the "View Our Archives" function, you will notice that this theme does indeed support that "template".

Go back to your dashboard, and lets choose another theme.

Another classic that I have used for ages for many sites is Hemingway by Kyle Neath.

Chapter 9 - Applying a theme

Current Theme

Hemingway by Kyle Neath

A staggered-column theme with excerpts on the front and a customizable footer.

OPTIONS: Widgets | Extras | Hemingway Options | Edit CSS

Tags: black, dark, custom colors, theme options, two columns, bottom widgets, fixed width

The bad part about using this blog on wordpress.com is you do not have access to your pages by default. So it may or may not be for you. I enjoy using it still, the contrast is beautiful, and it keeps you focused on the task at hand.

Go back to your dashboard, and lets choose another theme.

WordPress Foundations

This time we are going to pick another classic.

The theme is called "Unsleepable" by Ben Gray. If you are using the self-hosted version of WordPress, I highly recommend a customizable version of this called unwakeable. Lets activate the theme, and see how it looks.

Current Theme

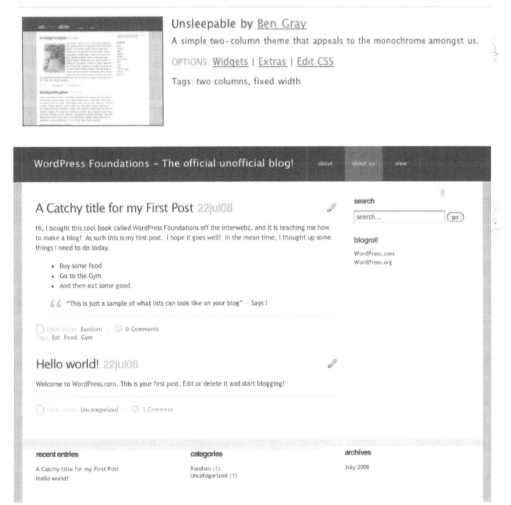

We have our "pages" at the top, and when you roll over the page, you will see it highlight (which is what I did to get this screen capture). You have your search, and on the bottom you have access to your archives, categories, and a quick list of recent entries.

This theme does not support our Archives Template. (Please note, this does not matter for us here, as there is no real reason to use an archive template page, when you have access to archives on your sidebar through a widget, which you can always add to your themes).

Go back to your dashboard, and lets choose one more theme.

Prologue.

This is a fun theme, I recommend it to friends who are trying to keep a nice little social blog, it is also cool for those who are working a project together, you can login, post and update and get back to work. I will show how this works, and create a custom entry via the front page of the blog!

The theme is called Prologue, it is by Joseph Scott, Matt Thomas, and Automattic (the makers of WordPress).

Current Theme

Prologue by Joseph Scott and Matt Thomas, Automattic
A group blog theme for short update messages, inspired by Twitter.

OPTIONS: Widgets | Extras | Custom Image Header | Edit CSS

Tags: blue, two columns, fixed width, custom header, microblog

WordPress Foundations - The official unofficial blog!

Hi, Anakin. Whatcha up to?

Tag it

Post it

Latest Updates RSS

Ani 5:44 pm on July 22, 2008 | **0** | # | e
Tags: **Eat**, **Food**, **Gym**

Hi, I bought this cool book called WordPress Foundations off the interwebz, and it is teaching me how to make a blog! As such this is my first post. I hope it goes well! In the mean time, I thought up some things I need to do today.

- Buy some food
- Go to the Gym
- And then eat some good.

"This is just a sample of what lists can look like on your blog" — Says I

Ani 4:41 am on July 22, 2008 | **1** | # | e

Welcome to **WordPress.com**. This is your first post. Edit or delete it and start blogging!

Recent Projects

Gym (1)   RSS
Food (1)   RSS
Eat (1)   RSS

All Updates RSS

Blog at WordPress.com
Prologue theme by **Automattic**

On the top of the screen you see your avatar, and you have the option to post an update to your blog about what you're doing, as well as providing some tags.

This theme does not make use of categories by default, so just post a tag. For example if your working on a game, you could write, engine coding, or skinning the characters, etc. This way you can click those tags and see the updates based on those tags from various users. If you had more than one user, they would show up as well and display their avatar.

WordPress Foundations - The official unofficial blog!

Hi, Anakin. Whatcha up to?

Testing out my cool new theme!

Tag it

new Theme!

Post it

Latest Updates RSS

Ani 5:44 pm on July 22, 2008 | **0** | # | **e**
Tags: **Eat, Food, Gym**

Hi, I bought this cool book called WordPress Foundations off the interwebz, and it is teaching me how to make a blog! As such this is my first post. I hope it goes well! In the mean time, I thought up some things I need to do today.

- Buy some food
- Go to the Gym
- And then eat some good.

"This is just a sample of what lists can look like on your blog" — *Says I*

Ani 4:41 am on July 22, 2008 | **1** | # | **e**

Welcome to **WordPress.com**. This is your first post. Edit or delete it and start blogging!

Recent Projects

Gym (1)   RSS
Food (1)   RSS
Eat (1)   RSS

All Updates RSS

Blog at WordPress.com
Prologue theme by **Automattic**

Here I'm filling out some information, as you can tell, I made a bad tag, I did this on purpose so we can delete the tag, and the post later on.

On the next page you can see what it looks like after you update the blog with your entry, you are never taken off the page, it is all done in real time, and quite smooth.

You can see the tags updated in real time as well.

Please note, when someone visits this site, they will not see "the ability to post on your blog", it will not appear, so no need to worry about people posting random stuff on your site, it is for users with logins only (to update their status).

WordPress Foundations - The official unofficial blog!

Hi, Anakin. Whatcha up to?

Tag it

Post it

Latest Updates 🔊 RSS

Ani 6:18 pm on July 22, 2008 | 0 | # | e
Tags: new Theme!

Testing out my cool new theme!

Ani 5:44 pm on July 22, 2008 | 0 | # | e
Tags: Eat, Food, Gym

Hi, I bought this cool book called WordPress Foundations off the interwebz, and it is teaching me how to make a blog! As such this is my first post. I hope it goes well! In the mean time, I thought up some things I need to do today.

- Buy some food
- Go to the Gym
- And then eat some good.

"This is just a sample of what lists can look like on your blog" -- Says I

Ani 4:41 am on July 22, 2008 | 1 | # | e

Welcome to **WordPress.com**. This is your first post. Edit or delete it and start blogging!

Recent Projects

new Theme! (1) 🔊 RSS
Gym (1) 🔊 RSS
Food (1) 🔊 RSS
Eat (1) 🔊 RSS

🔊 All Updates RSS

Blog at WordPress.com
Prologue theme by **Automattic**

We have gone over 5 different themes, discussed the pros and cons of each, its time to pick one to continue on with this course. Please note, these were just five that I recommend, and enjoy using.

If you decide to use the self-hosted version of WordPress on your sever, you will have access to THOUSANDS of themes.

Just remember, this is YOUR blog, do what you like, and express yourself. That's the only way to have fun.

I will continue using ChaoticSoul for this site.

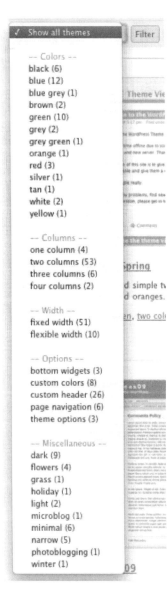

If you want a certain type of functionality for your theme, and looks come second, please take advantage of the drop down menu functionality that allows you to sort.

You can sort by color, how many columns, whether the columns are fixed (not resizable) or flexible (can resize based on the end users browser).

A few other really good themes you might want to check out are: Monotone, The Journalist, and cutline. These are a few other really good themes I recommend.

Chapter 10

Widgets

What Exactly Is a Widget?

Widgets are like plugins that allows you to quickly and easily customize your sidebar on your site by simply "dragging and dropping" the "widgets" into the preferred order you want them to show up as on your site.

Adding Widgets To Your Site

On your dashboard, on the left side menu click on Appearance then click Widgets. Every time you select a theme, be aware that each theme already has its on set of widgets pre set. Whenever you go into the widgets menu set, and add something, everything else gets erased on that theme (as far as widgets go, on your sidebar). It is a good idea to have your site open in a new window or tab prior to changing anything, so you can see where stuff was before you started messing with it.

It takes no time, and no skill to implement these widgets on your site. It is very fast to do, and the results are immediate.

You can revert back at anytime to "factory condition" specs by deleting the widgets you add to your site. When you do this, the default options will be restored.

Chapter 10 - Widgets

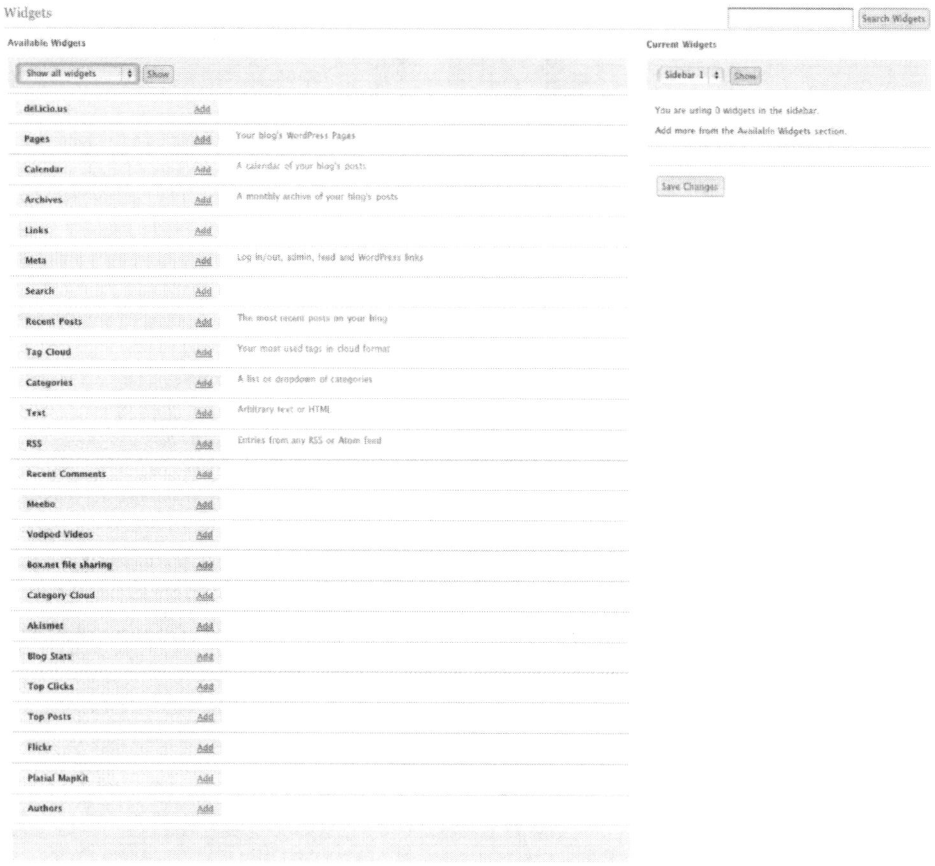

Widgets

On the right you will see your sidebar, you can use the drop down menu and select which sidebar you want to work with.

This particular theme has 1 sidebar others have 2 or more.

By Default, this theme has: Search, Pages, Archives, and Categories.

To add a widget, just click "add" and it will appear on the right.

When you add the widgets, you will see them as follows, you can click one by selecting the name, and drag it in the position you want it to appear on your blog.

Current Widgets

✓ Sidebar 1   Show

You are using 0 widgets in the sidebar.

Add more from the Available Widgets section.

Current Widgets

Sidebar 1 ⇕ Show

You are using 5 widgets in the sidebar.

Add more from the Available Widgets section.

Search	Edit
Calendar	Edit
Pages	Edit
Links	Edit
Text	Edit

Save Changes

Click "save changes" and then click view site to see how we did.

July 2008

S	M	T	W	T	F	S
		1	2	3	4	5
6	7	8	9	10	11	12
13	14	15	16	17	18	19
20	21	22	23	24	25	26
27	28	29	30	31		

PAGES

About

About Us

View our Archives

BLOGROLL

WordPress.com

WordPress.org

Here is the search feature.

This is the calendar, the bright white text, is showcasing something we have posted. When someone visits the site, they can scroll through the months, and click on bright white numbers to see what all you posted on that day.

Here are our various pages.

Here are the links, they can be changed by editing the blog roll (will be covered later).

Here is our textbox, which is missing because we have not typed anything in.

We now need to edit these widgets so they can provide more useful information.

With this theme, we cannot have prewritten text in the search, change the blog roll name, or the calendar.

We can add text, and give our "pages" a name.

You can use the text widget to input code (useful for ads).

Chapter 11

WordPress.com Extras & Upgrades

What is an extra?

This is a feature added for wordpress.com (only). Right now, it only provides two options, which we will cover now.

The first option is to Enable Snap Shots on your blog. What is this? Whenever you hover over a link, it will automatically preview that link, so you can see what it looks like prior to clicking it.

The second option of hiding related links on this blog, will take some time to talk about.

This feature is turned on by default (thus showing other related links on your blog). When you look at the bottom of a post, you will see "possible related posts" that are on other blogs on the wordpress.com domain.

If you leave this on, when someone visits your site, and enjoys an article, at the bottom they will get directed to another blog with similar content on the network, and as such away from you!

If you leave this on, then you get advertised on other blogs that have this feature turned on, so the choice is up to you. If you want to reach more people, you may want to leave this on, as it can only help. If you are running a business and it links to a competitor, well, that wouldn't be so good.

WordPress.com Upgrades

If you are using the self-hosted version of WordPress, you can skip this section and move on to the next chapter.

Upgrades, are additional features you can purchase for your wordpress.com blog. To view these features, go to your dashboard and choose upgrades (its at the bottom on the menu on the left).

A "Credit" is the form of currency for wordpress.com. Each Credit is equal to one dollar USD.

Custom CSS, lets you change the CSS of your blog, giving you much more creative control over how your blog looks.

Unlimited Private Users, means you can add more than 35 people to your blog.

The rest of your options are space upgrades, if your uploading a lot of files, such as photos and PDFs, you may need to upgrade your account to get more space (you have three gigs by default).

Gifts are for buying these items for other users on wordpress.com

The Domains option allows to you have your wordpress.com blog point to your domain. You are given the nameserver information to input on your domain name, so when a user types in yourblog.com, he does not see yourblog.wordpress.com.

This feature is 10 dollars a year, and is worth doing if you do not wish to pay for a hosting account, and want to keep your blog on WordPress.com.

You are not charged until the forwarding is working (at least at the time of this writing).

Chapter 12

Custom Image Header

Introduction to the Custom Image Header

Through the use of the "Custom Image Header" you can import your own graphics into the website and have them displayed at the top. (This is under Appearance)

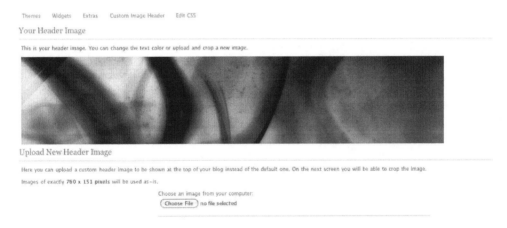

As you can see, you have the dimensions that you need for the theme, for this example it is 760 x 151.

This particular theme, will split the image in half, and show it on the two bars, so we need to make an image composition inside of Photoshop, gimp, or any of your favorite image editors.

If you were to upload an image larger than these dimensions you will be given the same menu you got before when you uploaded your avatar image. Lets start by adding a really large image, and cropping it in WordPress.

Click "choose an image from your computer" --> then select the jpg you want to add, then click Upload.

I will use the same image I posted before, to keep things simple.

Again, you want to choose part of your image, based on the "marching ants" or dotted lines in the rectangle.

Only resize from the corners (top left, top right, bottom left, bottom right,) as these will allow you to keep your dimensions and not skew your image.

When you are done, on the bottom click "Crop Header".

Themes   Widgets   Extras   Custom Image Header   Edit CSS

Header complete!

Visit your site and you should see the new header now.

You will be informed that the header has been cropped, and to go check your site to see how it looks.

So visit your site, and you see your header at the top.

As you can tell, this doesn't quite work with this theme. I will edit this photo in another application, to make it fit better with this theme.

I wrote out very detailed instructions, step by step on how to edit this photo, using the Internet, with no external application, meaning you can edit the photo anywhere in the world, on any kind of computer, all you need is internet access.

As this is a book about WordPress and not image manipulation, I'm not including that part in this book. However you sign up for my newsletter at EnlightenedWebmastery.com and get it there.

It is around 15-20 pages, and covers applying special effects (to tone down the image), and edit it so we can get the image to work with this theme (using 4 small images, opposed to 1 very large one).

I showcase each step, in detail, telling you why and how I went about creating the image, why I used the tools I did, and how to use them.

You can skip doing this if you want, it is not necessary, I just thought it would be useful to show how to do this for free, anywhere in the world, no experience necessary.

I should also note, it would be much simpler to do the whole effect in Photoshop or the gimp, but not everyone has those programs, or the desire to learn them.

Hence the completely free method I laid out in the book. Please check it out, and feel free to tell me what you think (besides the fact that the image does not go with this theme, which I will be changing back shortly).

Chapter 13

Custom Image Header Part 2

Putting up your custom header

In the special report you can get from my website, we went over a workflow for taking an image, manipulating it to better fit our design goals, and now we are ready to put this into our blog, as the official header.

Now, I already know this looks horrible, and is not the best example, but it was all I had on such short notice.

Go to your dashboard, and click on Appearance -> custom image header.

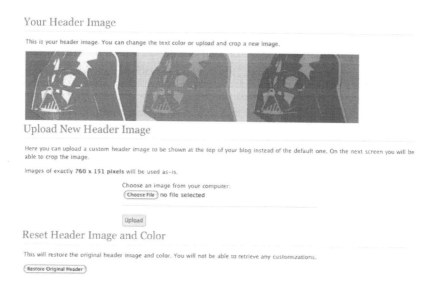

This is what our current image looks like, which is horrible too I might add. So what you need to do is click "choose file" and load up the new header you just saved in the special report. Then click upload. (If you want to revert back to the very beautiful image that was here before, click "restore original header" which will be doing soon!

Now you need to crop your photo, just as we did last time.

Choose the part of the image you want to use as your header.

Crop Header

When your finished, you will get a box saying "Header Complete", now go visit the site to see how it looks.

Here is what the site looks like now, much more subdued. If I was going to keep this image, I would make sure the links were changed from Yellow to a Carolina blue, and then it wouldn't look half bad.

The background would need to be changed to black, because brown and black do not work the best together. This cannot be done on wordpress.com, unless you pay to have CSS access.

You could also post a logo on the image where it shows your company, URL, whatever you want, and have that added to the image we uploaded.

Now I'm going to go back and click "restore original header" to get back to normal and we will continue on in the next chapter.

Chapter 14

Comments

Why Should I Enable Comments?

The main point of a blog in today's world is to communicate. When you post an article, and others read it, they like to share their insights with you, as well as other people. When they leave a post, it gives them incentive to check back to see what others wrote.

Someone could want to ask you a question about your post, or thank you, for helping him or her out with a problem.

For this reason I always recommend allowing comments, and to have them automatically posted. I go through a couple times a day checking for spam, and deleting posts that do not add to the discussion, I recommend you do the same.

Here is an example of how comments look on your blog.

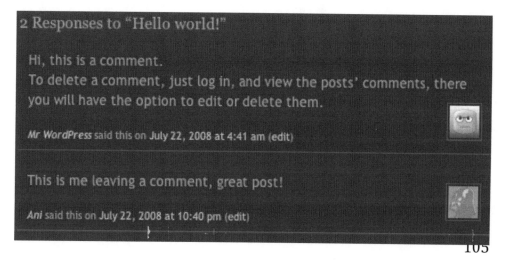

You need to be careful about your comments though, as I posted back in the chapter on writing posts, some people will try and spam your blog. One of the best things to do, is keep track of your comments, and delete anything that seems like spam.

If someone wrote that last post, I would definitely delete it! It adds nothing to the post. If he said Great Post, thanks, that would be different.

How to View Your Comments?

Go to your dashboard, and click comments. If you have the Recent Comments module running, you can also access your most recent ones from there.

You can see the users name, his website, and his email, in case you need to contact him. You can also see his post.

Hover over each comment and you will be able to approve a comment, you can mark it as spam, or you can delete it.

Comment

Submitted on 2008/07/22 at 10:40pm

This is me leaving a comment, great post!

Unapprove | Spam | Delete | Edit | Quick Edit | Reply

Submitted on 2008/07/22 at 4:01pm

hey, wow, what an amazing post!

Submitted on 2008/07/22 at 4:41am

Hi, this is a comment.
To delete a comment, just log in, and view the posts' cor

You can also decide to unapproved a comment, and get rid of it.

You can edit the post by clicking on it.

This is all you really need to know about comments. If you click on the "Akismet Spam" box you can check comments that the filter has picked up, this can ensure that no real comment accidently got tagged as spam. Spam is deleted automatically in 15 days.

Chapter 14 - Comments

Chapter 15

Adding Multimedia to your blog

What All Types of Multimedia Can I Add To My Blog

In today's age, you are no longer restricted to using just text on your website. You can make a blog full of pictures, videos, audio, and text. Adding these elements to your website used to require a good bit of technical know-how, and required a good bit of advanced trickery to get this to work on WordPress not so long ago. Now it is as simple as pointing and clicking!

How To Insert Images

Adding images to your articles, greatly improves the chances someone will read your post. It is less intimidating than a huge block of text, and very easy to accommodate. I will go over 2 different ways of how to add pictures, and share the pros and cons of each method.

First, we are going to add an image from amazon.com, and add it to our post.

Go to your dashboard, and write a new page, create a title, and insert some text.

I'm going to cheat, and use text from a review I wrote for a product on amazon.com.

Title

Adobe Photoshop Lightroom Review

Permalink: http://wpfoundations.wordpress.com/2008/07/23/adobe-photoshop-lightroom-1/ Edit

Post   Add media: ▣ ▢ ♫ ❋   Visual   HTML

B *I* ABC | ☰ ☰ ❝ | ☰ ☰ ☰ | ... | 🔗 🖻 ✂ ✏ ▾ □ ▦

Paragraph ▾ | U ▤ A ▾ | ▦ ▦ ⊘ Ω | ≢ ≢ | ↺ ↻ ◉

Adobe Lightroom is amazing. I have been using it since the first beta, it just wasn't something I could switch to. At a studio I work at they have Capture One, which is an amazing piece of software, but I found it lacking when it comes to organizing "my" photos. I bought Apples Aperture when it came out, and it blew me away. Aperture has the loupe, (now found in bridge cs3), light table (Lightrooms new compare feature), which is amazing for setting up comps, if you like to do story work on your photos. Aperture has a rejection tag that you can use to reject photos to delete later (bad blur, or too many like shots), Lightroom now has this feature as well--you just press X, then when you are ready to rid yourself of those click the delete rejected photos button, if you rejected it accidentally press U, if you have a favorite pic just press P to "pick" it. Aperture has stacks, which if you shoot multiple exposures (hdr, pano, etc) they can be stacked up and you can choose a pick, Lightroom in version 1 now has this as well. The other big feature any other raw program needs to compete with Aperture for me is their collections. Its similar to a smart playlist in iTunes, you can sort by rating, keyword, what have you. Lightroom now has this as well, meaning you can pick your favorite waterfall photos from several years of shooting and put them in a logical folder, meaning no extra space to store your favorites. This feature, and rejection caused me to loose over 40gb by switching to Lightroom!

While my review may seem as though Lightroom copied the best features from Aperture and improved upon them, for the most part that's true. The best part is they improved soo many other features. If you have used Aperture, or iPhoto, you know how big a joke their clone stamp tool is. Lightroom? Just as good as Photoshop! I'm constantly changing lens when I'm out in the field

Path: p

If I go ahead and preview this post (by clicking preview), you can see how uninteresting it looks as pure text.

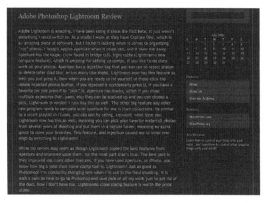

Now, to add in some pictures, in the visual editor, move your mouse to the location where you want to add a picture, then click on the insert / edit image option.

Put the URL in. Give it a descriptive name. Give the Image a Caption. Choose how you want to align the text to the image. Then click Insert into post.

This is a very large image, and doesn't look the way I want, so lets change it.

Highlight the image, and click the "Edit Image" button.

 You can dynamically adjust the image based on percentage and let WordPress calculate the dimensions for you, while keeping track of how it looks in the preview above.

If you want to change it more, click advanced, and type in a smaller number, then click update.

Here, I change it to 250x250, and click update.

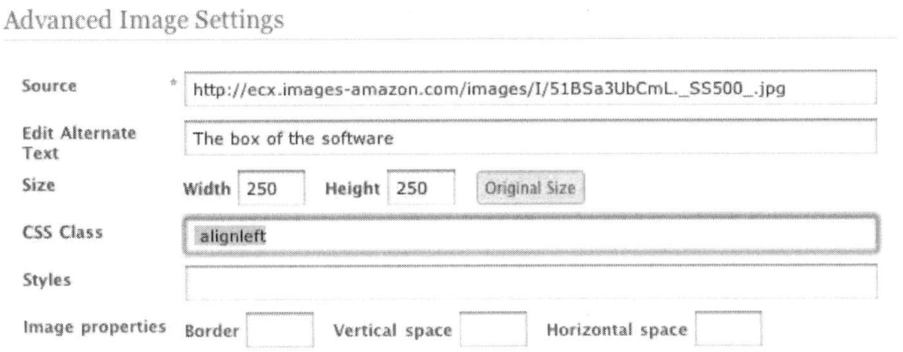

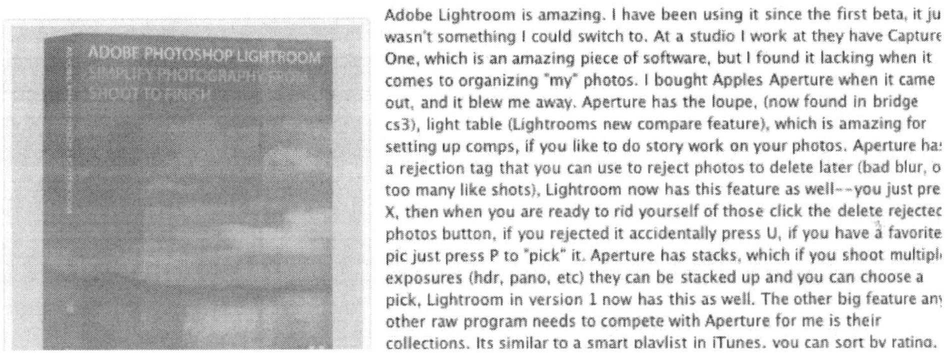

This is much better, but still to large, I think one more time will do it!

In the next image you can see that I moved the slider down to 60% and it made it even smaller, in this case, 150x150. I think it looks much better.

I think you will agree, this is much more manageable.

Adding Images Throughout the Body of Your Article

Lets show another way to do this, and go over adding an image using an alternate alignment.

Advanced Image Settings

Source	* http://images.amazon.com/images/G/01/software/detail-page/featuretour.jpg	
Edit Alternate Text		
Size	Width 173 Height 110 Original Size	
CSS Class	alignright	
Styles	margin-left: 10px; margin-right: 10px; margin-top: 5px; margin-bottom: 5px;	
Image properties	Border Vertical space Horizontal space	

This image is right aligned, and I adjusted the alignment, adding some vertical and horizontal space to get it to look better in the post.

Advanced Image Settings

Source	* http://images.amazon.com/images/G/01/software/detail-page/testimonials.jpg	
Edit Alternate Text		
Size	Width 203 Height 144 Original Size	
CSS Class	alignleft	
Styles	margin-left: 10px; margin-right: 10px; margin-top: 5px; margin-bottom: 5px;	
Image properties	Border Vertical space Horizontal space	

On this image, I left aligned it, lowered the size of the image, and set the vertical space to 5 and put the horizontal at 10. This gives it some nice space around the image.

Here is what the final post looks like, adding 3 images. I think it reads better.

The second way of adding an image, is uploading an image from your computer, and inserting it onto your blog.

If you are going to be uploading photos that you just took with your digital camera, I encourage you to use some software to reduce the size of those images; 1200x1200 should be the largest any image should be for the web.

The images on this post are all under 200x200, this is why it is not so large. Set it so that when the user clicks on the image, it can load up the fuller sized image. I suggest trying to keep the image size down to 700 pixels wide (or much less). Unless your making a photoblog, there is no need in having such a large size for an image, as it makes the viewer wait longer to load up your page, and the longer they wait, the sooner they will just walk away.

You can upload your photos from your digital camera to Photoshop, and adjust the image size, and save that (or upload to a flickr account, and link to your image on your blog).

I'm going to add my picture under the about me page, and show how to do it.

In your dashboard, click Pages -> Edit -> then click About Us.

In your post choose a spot, and click the insert image.

Click on the "choose files to upload", and select your image.

Fill in the information as necessary.

I'm leaving the link URL in there, with that being there, you can click on the image to view the image in full size.

Click insert into post, and now it will be on your page.

The image is quite large, so lets go back and adjust the size the way we did before.

I had to make this quite small to get it work right. Here are the settings, and the final output.

Edit Image | Advanced Settings

Size	
130%	
120%	
110%	
100%	
90%	
80%	
70%	
60%	

Advanced Image Settings

Source: http://wpfoundations.wordpress.com/files/2008/07/me-small-300-black.jpg?w=214

Edit Alternate Text: The Author

Size: Width 50 Height 70 [Original Size]

CSS Class: size-medium wp-image-20 alignright

Styles:

Image properties: Border Vertical space Horizontal space

About Us

 We created this course to give users a proper foundational level of knowledge on learning how to use, and understand wordpress. We think these are the pure essentials anyone must know in order to go forward in using wordpress. There is always more to learn, but with this in your hands, you can accomplish most any task that is laid out before you.

Warning about adding images to your website.

When you are adding images to your blog, you need to make sure that you own the copyright to that image, or that it is in the public domain, or is copyright free.

If you want to make sure you get images you can post on your website (news sites are generally a safe bet). You can buy photos from *http://www.istockphoto.com* or check out the following site for free images.

http://search.creativecommons.org/

Of further note, please understand, when you are linking your images from another website (opposed to hosting them on your own site) your stealing that persons bandwidth, which is not nice at all, and if the website changes the name of the image, or deletes it, your site will have missing images, and can confuse people, as it is unlikely you will notice that this has happened.

Adding Video From Youtube.com

You can add video the same way you added the image previously, you do so by clicking the "add video" button.

Go to YouTube.com, and find a video that you enjoy, and copy the URL (you cannot use the embed code on wordpress.com, so use the URL). Please note if you are using wordpress.org, you can use the embed code.

Click "Add Video" then Input the URL, and click insert into post.

Insert some text, and then click publish (note that I changed the permalink, and added tags).

Tip about uploading videos

Whenever you want to share a video, you cannot upload it to your server using wordpress.com, if you have your own server you can, but you need to compress it very highly so it does not take long to download.

A good idea is to go sign up at youtube.com and upload your video there, and then you can link to it here on your blog.

The benefit to this is it eats up YouTube's bandwidth, opposed to your own. And they will have it backed up for all of eternity, no chance in loosing it (so do not post something you do not ever want seen!).

How to add audio to your blog

You have two different ways to implement audio into your blog. The first way fixes it so the user clicks a link, and can download the audio, or is launched automatically into the users default Internet audio player. The second way is to "embed" the audio into your site, and allow users to play your audio via a flash player, while staying on your site.

I prefer both methods, I create audio streams for users to listen to, as well as a "download" link.

This is amazing if your creating a blog for your local church or college, as you can have classes posted up and the students can check out the audio from the webpage, without having to download anything, or use any other software. Which is especially useful in a locked down environment.

To add the audio via a player, just type in [audio http://www.domain.com/song.mp3].

While you are writing up your post, click insert audio, and type out the following (replace spooky with what matters, I changed it to download).

Chapter 15 - Adding Multimedia to your blog

Choose File Gallery (0) Media Library

From Computer

Allowed file types: jpg, jpeg, png, gif, pdf, doc, ppt, odt.

Choose files to upload

You are using the Flash uploader. Problems? Try the Browser uploader instead.

179.3 kB used, 3.0 GB (100.0%) upload space remaining. You can upload additional file types and increase your available space with a Space Upgrade.

— OR —

From URL

Audio File URL * http://soundrangers.com/free-sound-effects/spooky04.mp3

Title   * Spooky

Link text, e.g. "Still Alive by Jonathan Coulton"

Insert into Post

Type this into your blog.

Title

Adding audio to your wordpress blog

Permalink: http://wpfoundations.wordpress.com/2008/07/23/ spooky-mp3 / Save Cancel

Post   Add media: 🔲 🖼 🎵 ✳   Visual   HTML

B *I* ABC ≔ ≣ ❝ ▤ ▤ ▤ ∞ ✂ ▤ ✇ ▾ ▢ ▦

Paragraph ▾ **U** ▤ A ▾ ▦ ▦ ∅ Ω ⇥ ⇤ ↺ ↻ ⓘ

Adding MP3 to your blog

[audio http://soundrangers.com/free-sound-effects/spooky04.mp3]

Download

When you are finished, it will look like this when published.

Just as with video, you cannot upload audio to your wordpress.com account. As such you will need to host it on an external server (you can use free webhosting, and link to that file, but shhhhh).

Managing your Media Library

When you add images, or other files, WordPress will automatically keep track of them, and organize them. It does not list what you have linked to (images, YouTube videos, mp3's, etc), only that which you personally uploaded, it will show up here.

You can filter, and search by type or name, and delete it if you need to free up some space.

If you click the item, you will see more information about it, and it will tell you what all posts it appears on, and any comments on the item.

You can add other files on your blog, such as PDF files, or PowerPoint presentations. The choice is yours, you do it the same way as shown here, the only difference is WordPress does not present the material in any special way. It creates a link just as it did when you added the mp3 file.

Remember, you access your media library by clicking the Media button on the left hand side menu on your dashboard, and choose Library.

Chapter 16

Managing Your Pages and Posts

Introduction to the More Tag

In a previous chapter, we posted a long review on our blog. The problem is, when you pull up the website, people have to look at that large body of text, and scroll around. As such they may decide to leave the site than deal with having to view that large body of text. This is where the More Tag comes in.

Have you noticed when you visit a blog, the home page says, to read the rest of the post, click here. This is the beauty of the More Tag.

Applying The More Tag

Go to your dashboard, under Posts, choose Edit, and select the post that has the large body of text.

What we need to do now, is write a summary, or a brief introductory paragraph for the article, and follow with the more tag.

The more tag is the first button.

When your through, and click the "more tag" button, you will see the graphic below, click save, and visit the site.

Title

Adobe Photoshop Lightroom Review

Permalink: http://wpfoundations.wordpress.com/2008/07/22/adobe-photoshop-lightroom-1/ Edit

Post   Visual   HTML

The name of this program is, Adobe Lightroom. I have been using it since beta, and I have to say, it brings serious joy to my life.

The program has a very deep and easy to use "tagging" system, which allows me to sort not only by name, or by a keyword, but I can also search by which lens or camera body, the date, and I can assign a color, and sort by that on an image by image basis. You can sort by ISO, your fstop, or your shutter speed. It is incredible.

Please read on to find out how Lightroom caused me to loose over 40GB of wasted space in under a day!

More...

Path: p

This is what the front page of the blog looked like, prior to implementing the more tag.

I had to make the text extremely small to get it all to fit on my large monitor.

Here is what the front page post now looks like now that we used the more tag:

Adobe Photoshop Lightroom Review July 23, 2008 • No Comments (Edit)

Hey, I just found this really cool photo editing program. It is made by Adobe (the makers of Photoshop), what it does is organize all of your photos, and lets you work with raw photo files in real time, and allows quick and easy access to manipulate them.

The name of this program is, Adobe Lightroom. I have been using it since beta, and I have to say, it brings serious joy to my life.

The program has a very deep and easy to use "tagging" system, which allows me to sort not only by name, or by a keyword, but I can also search by which lens or camera body, the date, and I can assign a color, and sort by that on an image by image basis. You can sort by ISO, your fstop, or your shutter speed. It is incredible.

Please read on to find out how Lightroom caused me to loose over 40GB of wasted space in under a day!

Continue reading 'Adobe Photoshop Lightroom Review'

Learning how to use the excerpt tag

This is great, but when you search by archive, you will still see the introductory post, prior to the more tag, what we need to do now, is write a quick excerpt about the article, so when it is searched for, they see that piece of information opposed to the introduction (especially if it is long like this is.)

I like to keep these at around 25 words, very short, and to the point, with keywords so when users are searching, they can easily find the post.

Go back to your dashboard, click manage, then post, and scroll down to bottom of your post. To the advanced section, you will see excerpt, click it open, and follow along.

Here is an example of an appropriate excerpt for the article.

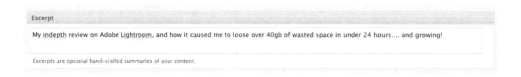

Our current theme does not display any information when you search, or use the archives, other than the title.

When you switch back to Kubrick, you see what is before the more tag.

Archive for the 'Review' Category

Adobe Photoshop Lightroom Review
July 23, 2008

Hey, I just found this really cool photo editing program. It is made by Adobe (the makers of Photoshop), what it does is organize all of your photos, and lets you work with raw photo files in real time, and allows quick and easy access to manipulate them.

The name of this program is, Adobe Lightroom. I have been using it since beta, and I have to say, it brings serious joy to my life.

The program has a very deep and easy to use "tagging" system, which allows me to sort not only by name, or by a keyword, but I can also search by which lens or camera body, the date, and I can assign a color, and sort by that on an image by image basis. You can sort by ISO, your fstop, or your shutter speed. It is incredible.

Please read on to find out how Lightroom caused me to loose over 40GB of wasted space in under a day!

(more...)

When you switch to digg 3 columns, you get to see the excerpt.

Adobe Photoshop Lightroom Review

Posted on July 23, 2008 by Ani | Edit

My indepth review on Adobe Lightroom, and how it caused me to loose over 40gb of wasted space in under 24 hours.... and growing!

Filed under: Review | Tagged: adobe, lightroom, photoshop, Review | No Comments »

So again, this is based on your theme, but this is such a good habit to get into, that it is worth doing it.

I do not like having duplicate content on my sites, and using the excerpt function, along with the more tag, and having different content on all 3 pages, ensures this is kept to the minimum. The reason I do not like duplicate content, is for SEO reasons.

Deleting and Editing Content

If a post of yours didn't go over so well and you wish to delete it, or edit it, that is what we are going to cover in this section.

Say you run a celebrity gossip blog, and your favorite celebrity couple just had twins, you write up a post, and then later on when the names are announced, you can edit your post and add that information (and make a separate post of course), as well as add in some pictures (and link to your newer posts).

To do this you need to use the edit function.

In your dashboard, click on Posts, then Edit. Select a post you want to edit by clicking the title.

After you have made your changes (whatever they may be), read the text and make sure everything is right.

Take the time to read over your post, and make sure it covers everything, you see no glaring mistakes, both spelling wise, and grammar wise. Once you are happy, click save. Your post is now edited, and will appear exactly where it was (chronologically).

If you want the edited post to appear as the latest entry on your blog, you need to do the following.

On the right side of your window, where you click save, you will see a dialog box like the one below, all you need to do is adjust the date to the current time, and date, and then click save. The post will magically be brought up to the front of your blog (I do not recommend this, but I am mentioning it in case you want too.)

When you edit your posts it is a good habit to write on the bottom of the post that you edited it, and why you edited it.

For example you could write:

"UPDATE 7/28/08, Brad Pitt's new kids name is _____.

Be sure to check back on my blog for the latest happenings!

Click this link to read the latest news on this story."

Chapter 17

Categories and Tags

The difference between categories and tags

The major difference between categories and tags are, categories are more general. If your writing a blog on video games, and your covering home gaming systems (consoles), you would make a category on Xbox 360, and you would make a tag on Halo 3, because unless you are a Halo 3 fansite, you are more likely to cover other games, opposed to just one. This allows you to have many posts about Halo 3, and have posts about other games too. If a user visits your website, he can now choose to look at all Xbox 360 posts, and see all the various games. If he wants to check out more on that particular game, all he has to do is click the tag, and he will see all posts you have made with that tag. It's a beautiful thing, and a wonderful addition to WordPress.

Creating Your Categories

Now that you know why categories are so important, lets go ahead and cover how to create them in bulk through the dashboard.

Open up your dashboard, click on Posts, then choose categories.

Chapter 17 - Categories and Tags

You can see the categories you have on your current blog.

Here's a snapshot of a blog I setup, that has some more descriptive categories, it is for a photography blog. The interface is different because it is using an older version of WordPress, and is self-hosted opposed to run on wordpress.com.

Take note of the detailed descriptions, and how they relate to the category name. This blog was created before we had tags.

7	Canon	Articles written for or about Canon DSLR's. This will cover guides, faqs, how to's and help.	0	0	Edit	Delete
4	Lightroom	Articles written about Adobe Photoshop Lightroom. These can consist of workflows, tips, guides, as well as FAQS.	0	0	Edit	Delete
8	Photo	This is where I post Photo's. You can view any of my photos that I have posted to the blog. Most will be posted on Flickr, and shown here.	30	0	Edit	Delete
6	Photography	This will cover photographic tips, such as compositing, and helpful ideas.	0	0	Edit	Delete
5	Photoshop	Articles written for Adobe Photoshop. Mainly the current version CS3.	0	0	Edit	Delete
3	Reviews	Reviews of software, hardware, games, books and videos.	0	0	Edit	Delete
1	Uncategorized		0	0	Edit	Default

To add a category, just type in the name, and insert the information presented.

Add Category

Category Name

The name is used to identify the category almost everywhere, for example under the post or in the category widget.

Category Parent

None

Categories, unlike tags, can have a hierarchy. You might have a Jazz category, and under that have children categories for Bebop and Big Band. Totally optional.

Description

This description is not prominent by default, however some themes may show it.

Add Category

Give your category a name.

Earlier we talked about the differences between tags and categories, and how you should be general in your category name, and much more specific when it comes to your tags.

Unlike tags, you will always be able to see the categories you have, as such, try and keep them to a minimum.

The Category Parent is what you would select if you wanted to subdivide your categories.

Earlier in this book I mentioned an example using video games, to continue on in that theme, you could create a "parent category" of "Consoles", and then make children of, Xbox 360, Playstation 3, and Nintendo Wii.

This way, if a user had all three systems, he could select Consoles, and see all your console related news, but if he only had a Wii, he could select that tag, and see only Nintendo Wii posts.

Then you need to give a description. Look at the previous picture, and see how the descriptions were made, make it simple, you're not writing an article, try and keep it between one and two sentences.

You can go ahead and create as many categories right now as you want, when you are finished, we will go over tags some more, and show exactly how to manage them, and a cool little tool that can make tags even more fun!

Adding Tags

Adding tags are very simple.

From your dashboard, click on Posts, then select Tags.

Scroll down below your actual post, and you will see the "tags" menu box. Here is where you select your tags.

You really need to try and be consistent; WordPress does not let you see visually all the tags you have on your site while your writing your post.

In keeping with the video game theme, try not to use Xbox, Xbox 360, and Xbox360, choose one, and stick to it, or use all three if you want too, the point is to be consistent.

Deleting Tags

If your looking over a post, and do not like that tag, you can delete it by clicking the little x button next to the name.

Managing your tags

Say you have had your blog for a while now, and you're trying to organize your tags. This little sample site we have been creating here, has no purpose, and only a few posts, yet the amount of tags are already becoming unruly. We currently have 15 tags, in as few as three or four posts.

You may be wondering how you can start consolidating tags, and getting rid of them if needed.

Inside of your dashboard, click on Posts, then choose Tags, and you will see the following screen.

Chapter 17 - Categories and Tags

Whenever you click on "quick edit" you can choose to rename your tag, doing so makes changes site wide, so if you accidently misspelled a tag, and have been doing so for quite some time, you can easily change it, and it will be as though it never happened.

If you decide you no longer want the tag, just delete it, and it is gone. Click the little checkbox, and choose delete (its near the top).

If you want to see what all posts you have that are using that tag, click the number on the right that shows how many posts you have with it, and you will be presented with a dialog box similar to this one.

From here you can check your stats, the other tags on that post, and if you have any comments.

Manage Posts tagged with "ghost ride the whip"   [   ] [Search Posts]

All Posts | Published (6)

[Delete] [Show all dates ⇕] [View all categories ⇕] [Filter]

☐	Date	Title	Author	Categories	Tags		Status	Stats
☐	23 hours ago	Grandma is Ghost Riding the Whip	Ani	Random	video, grandma, ghost ride the whip		Published	☑

Converting your categories to tags

If you have had your WordPress blog for sometime, you may have quite the collection of categories. Thanks to the recent update, you now have tags built in, and after seeing how useful they are, you might want to change your categories to tags.

Doing this is very easy. Load up your dashboard, click on Tools, and choose Import. Then click **Categories to Tags Converter**.

Dashboard ▾	(Categories to Tags) (Tags to Categories)
Dashboard	
Blog Stats	🔧 *Convert Categories (4) to Tags.*
Blog Surfer	
My Comments	Hey there. Here you can selectively convert existing categories to tags. To get started, check the categories you wish to be converted, then click the
Tag Surfer	Convert button.
Readomatic	Keep in mind that if you convert a category with child categories, the children become top-level orphans.
Posts ▾	
Edit	(Check All)
Add New	
Tags	☐ Gym (1)
Categories	☐ Random (4)
Media ▾	☐ Review (1) *
Library	☐ Uncategorized (1)
Add New	* This category is also a tag. Converting it will add that tag to all posts that are currently in the category.
Links	
Pages ▾	(Convert Categories to Tags)
Edit	
Add New	
Comments ❶	

All you need to do is click a category, and select convert selection to tags.

Convert your Tags to Categories

From the same screen as above, select "Tags to Categories".

Categories to Tags | Tags to Categories

Convert Tags (15) to Categories.

Here you can selectively converts existing tags to categories. To get started, check the tags you wish to be converted, then click the Convert button.

The newly created categories will still be associated with the same posts.

Check All

- adobe (1)
- audio (1)
- download (1)
- Eat (1)
- Food (1)
- ghost ride the whip (1)
- grandma (1)
- ☑ Gym (1)
- lightroom (1)
- mp3 (1)
- new Theme! (1)
- photoshop (1)
- Review (1) *
- spooky (1)
- video (1)

* This tag is also a category. When converted, all posts associated with the tag will also be in the category.

Convert Tags to Categories

Select the "Tags" you wish to convert into a Category (you can select more than one), and press "Convert".

Categories to Tags   Tags to Categories

- Converting tag **Gym** ... Converted successfully.

We're all done here, but you can always convert more.

Now you're finished. If you find you are constantly using a tag, and you think you should convert it to a category, this is how.

If you find out your not using as a category as much as you thought you would, you can convert it to a tag.

Chapter 17 - Categories and Tags

Chapter 18

Adding Users

Introduction to adding users

For a personal blog, it is unlikely you will want to add users to your blog, as the users we add to the blog enables them to post content. **So feel free to skip this chapter** if you do not think you will be adding them.   For the rest of us, the benefit of having more than one user is, you do not have to do all the work.

Say your making a website for your church, or any other local organization.   You can give several members, varying levels of access to the blog, from being able to add content, to being able to having full control of the blog.

Another good reason to have more users, is if your running a news site, or a fansite, and you want to post several updates. If you look at any major blog, you will see content provided by various authors.

When you are given an account, or give someone else an account on your WordPress blog, they will be a contributor.

Meaning you can login; write up a post, and boom, your done. It is not published on the blog, but the owner or an editor can login and choose to publish your post (ensuring it is of good quality), once you have been a member of that blog for a while, you may get promoted so you can just start publishing as soon as you are finished writing the post. WordPress gives you this level of flexibility, and is not something to take lightly!

The Different user classes

I am listing these in order of privileges allowed. From most restricted to least.

Contributor - This guy can login to your blog, write some posts, as well as edit (their own posts), can upload files to the blog.

They cannot publish their posts; those have to be published by a user of higher class.

Author - This guy can do everything the contributor can, plus he can post and delete his own posts.

Editor - This guy can do everything the author can, and he can edit other people's posts, publish unpublished posts, edit comments, pretty much everything you could want, in regards to managing content. This person needs to be someone you can trust, as he can pretty much control all the content on the blog.

Administrator - He can do any and everything, including deleting the blog.

Inviting a user

To invite a user, go to your WordPress dashboard, click the Users option, and choose **invites**. You can choose the class, and decide if you want to add them to your blog roll (list of links you can post on your site), or to add them as a contributor.

Once they get your email, they need to join WordPress, using the same steps we did earlier on in this book.

A screenshot of adding a user

Managing Users

To manage your users, just go to your dashboard, click users. When you do this you will see your users, if you have many users, you can sort by class, or type in their name in the search box.

You can see how many posts they have made, as well as remove them from your blog (click the check box).

If you wish to promote the user, just click their name, and then you can promote or demote them based on the list we discussed earlier.

Chapter 19

Password Protection

Why do I want to password protect?

Some reasons you may want to password protect a page are as follows:

- Creating an event you only want select people to know and communicate about.

- A special offer for certain people.

- A promotion.

- You want to sell some information, and have that information given only to those with the password.

- To share embarrassing photos with someone.

What can go wrong using password protection?

As with anything, people like to share. You have to realize that people will share the password with friends, family, or the whole Internet! So do not rely on password protection for something really important.

The way this works is, you create a password, and you give that password out to people. Those people visit your post, and type in the password in order to gain access.

How to protect a page or post using a password

Go to your dashboard, click Pages, then Edit, and choose a Page. At the top where it says Publish, under visibility, select "Password Protected".

Whenever someone visits your site, they will see the title, when they click on it, they will have to type in the password, when they do, they will be able to see the content.

You can still see the Page listed below (About Us). When you click on it, you will be asked to input the password.

Protected: About Us

 We created this course to give users a proper foundational level of knowledge on learning how to use, and understand wordpress. We think these are the pure essentials anyone must know in order to go forward in using wordpress. There is always more to learn, but with this in your hands, you can accomplish most any task that is laid out before you.

When you finish typing in the password, you will be allowed to view the page, as above.

How to get rid of Password Protection

Go back to your dashboard, click manage, and select either page or post depending on what you chose prior, and delete the password from the page.

Now when you view the site, the password is no longer required.

Chapter 19 - Password Protection

Chapter 20

Your Blog roll

Introduction to Blog Rolls

So, you may have wondered what a "blog roll" is, and why you have one or need one.

When you find a website you enjoy, and you want to share it with the world, you can add it to your blog roll. Then readers on your blog will see the link, and can decide to check it out. That site may add you to their blog roll as well. It's a great way to communicate with your audience, and helps to grow your community.

You are not stuck to having just one "blog roll", you can create multiple lists that are separate. For example, you can have a list of friends, stores, sites, services, family, etc.

Adding Links

In your dashboard, click on Links (left side menu), then "Add New".

You're given three options. The Name (this will show up on your blog roll), the address (this needs to be the complete URL including http://), and a description (what users will see when they are hovering over your link, provided snapshotz are not enabled).

You can flesh this out, by assigning categories to your links. Make sure you hit save after you add the link.

After adding these in, you can see how it looks on your site by clicking visit site (after hitting save).

If you decide you want to delete some links, just go to Links -> Edit, from your dashboard.

Chapter 21

Maintenance

Introduction To Maintenance

If you are running a business website, where your information is more static than dynamic, you may not need to create much content, as most of your material will be static. For others who are interested in keeping a content filled blog, you need to create some content regularly, as well as do some basic "house keeping".

Posting Content

Google loves sites that have new content. Google actually ranks higher based on the "freshness" of your content. Meaning the more often you update your blog, with valuable content, the more often it will get indexed, and the higher you will rank. This is important, because the higher you are ranked, the more people that can view your website and buy whatever your selling, or respond to your latest news articles.

A good rule is to make an update at least once a week if you can, more if possible, but try and be consistent.

When you are first starting out your blog, it's a good habit to post every day for some time (at least a month or so) then you can drop down to 2-3 times a week, you can go lower as needed (but try to at least update once a week), this way your site becomes more valuable, and your readers will thank you.

How can I keep creating fresh content?

People enjoy hearing about the latest news on whatever it is your covering. They want to know about the latest celebrity babies, and newest white house scandal, and who is sleeping with who. A good idea would be keep apprised on the information in your particular community (niche), and providing relevant content as necessary.

Check your comments and trackbacks

Everyday I check my comments and trackbacks (or try to) and I suggest you do the same. This doesn't take as long as you think it may (5-10 minutes, even on a popular blog).

Checking and deleting your spam.

Try and manually delete your spam, check it daily to see what's going on, and be on top of things.

Checking your incoming links.

See who is linking to you, check out their blog, and maybe leave a comment for them to read, or email them to show your appreciation.

Look for news and updates in the WordPress community.

At least once a week, pay attention to the news updates on your dashboard, and see what's going on in the community.

Check your stats.

See how many visitors your getting, the keywords they searched to come to your site, and the articles they enjoy the most, this way you can adapt to provide better content for your users.

Chapter 22

Self-Hosted Bloggers

Where Do I Get WordPress.org

Visit _wordpress.org_, on the home page you will see a button telling you to download.

What do I need to install it?

You need a web server (hosting account), and you need FTP access to that server.

You need a text editor (to open a php file).

A FTP client to connect to your server (windows users download filezilla, os x users use Cyberduck).

A web browser so you can set up and configure the installation.

How to install wordpress.org in under 5 minutes

After you download WordPress, decompress it, and rename the file wp-config-sample.php to wp-config.php, then open it up in your text editor.

Put in your information for your database, ex:

```
define('DB_NAME', 'WordPress');    // The name of the database
define('DB_USER', 'username');        // Your MySQL username
define('DB_PASSWORD', 'password');    //    ...and    password
define('DB_HOST', 'localhost');    // 99% chance you won't need to
change this value
```

Proceed with uploading the files to your server.

I.e. If you want it to be yourdomain.com you would upload all the files inside the WordPress directory to your root directory on your server (not the WordPress folder itself), if you wanted it to be in another folder, like yourname.com/wp/ then rename the WordPress folder to wp, and upload the folder to your server.

How to create a MySQL database and user

There are many ways, I'm going to cover using phpmyadmin.

Login to your phpmyadmin dashboard.

MySQL DB Wizard

MySQL Management	
MySQL	▶

The MySQL Database Creation Wizard Step 1

The first step of the MySQL database creation wizard allows you to create a database. In the Name of database field enter the name of the database you are creating. This name will be used later when you connect to the database from any database client or tool. The Database description field allows you to provide a short description of the database. This description is used only in the control panel to remind you of the purpose of this database.

Name of database	testing ✛
Database description	its a test!

?!	Next

Give your database a name (write this down) and give it a description, then click Next.

MySQL DB Wizard

⊘ **Information:** Database ___testing has been created successfully

The MySQL Database Creation Wizard Step 2. Adding Users to mistafr_testing

In this step you will add users and set their privileges on the newly created database. In the left part of the form you can add new users. In the right part you can set privileges for already existing users on the newly created database. To add a new user, enter the user login and password, then select a typical role for this user. If you need to set more specific privileges, you can do this from the "MySQL privileges" form later (after the user has been created). To set privileges on the newly created database for an existing user, select this user from the list, then select a typical role of this user and then press the "Add existing user" button. If you need to set more specific privileges on the database, you can do this from the "MySQL privileges" form later.

Add MySQL user to the database mistafr_testing

User name	itsauser ✛
Password	•••••• ✛
Confirm password	•••••• ✛
User role	read/write ⬍
	Add user

	Finish

Give yourself a username and password, write these down, as you need to add these to your wp-config.php file.

Now you can upload your file via FTP.

If you get a database error problem, you need to edit your profile, your hostname might need to be changed, or you could have mistyped something. You might need to change the permissions on your server (check online for the right ones for you).

Where to get free themes for your blog

As of July 18th, WordPress is bringing back the theme database, and is now open for new submissions; expect to see it grow astronomically.

Check it out here - *http://wordpress.org/extend/themes/*

When you search for a theme, you will see something similar to the following:

Extend Home

Plugins

Themes

- Upload Theme
- My Themes
- More Info
- Contact Us

Ideas

Kvetch!

Popular Tags More »

fixed width (24)

widgets (16)

two columns (15)

blue (13)

white (12)

Barthelme

Description Stats

Author: scottwallick

A minimalist theme where white space
and margins show culture and
aestheticism. For WordPress 2.6.x.

Tags: variable width, fixed width, two columns, widgets, theme options, options
page, white, gray, typography, microformats, hatom, hcard

Download

Preview

FYI

Version: 4.6

Last Updated: 2008-07-19

Author Homepage »

Theme Homepage »

Average Rating

☆☆☆☆☆
(4 ratings)
See what others are saying...

If the screenshot interests you, click on "Preview" and you get to
see it live. If you like it, click "download".

How do I install themes?

Once you have the file downloaded, you can decompress it, and get
in your ftp program, login, go to your wp-content folder, and you
want to put your theme folder under themes, if it requires plugins
you put those plugins under the plugins folder.

Make sure you upload the folder, not the root directory (files).

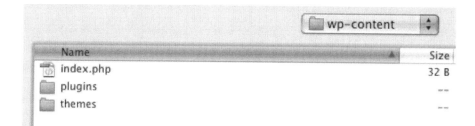

Name	Size
index.php	32 B
plugins	--
themes	--

Chapter 22 - Self-Hosted Bloggers

Chapter 23

Where To Go From Here

Continuing Your Journey

By now you know how to get your blog up and running. You know how to make posts, you have a schedule for when to do what to keep your blog healthy. You know how to change themes. Basically, you know all you really need to know to use WordPress.

You may be wondering what's next, how can I take my newfound skills, enhance them, and start making a profit, or getting more and more traffic to my website.

The only thing you really need to concern yourself with now is Blogging Strategies, and some more advanced techniques for "Mastering The Web", such as SEO, PPC, content creation, lead generation, Analytics, optimization, and more.

Introducing Enlightened WebMastery

The point behind Enlightened WebMastery, is for me to take what I have spent "YEARS!" of my life learning, and thousands of dollars on learning, narrowing it down into something you can apply right away, and get results. Without requiring you to go through the same pain, getting ripped off, or having to be afraid of not knowing which way to go next (and usually end up going nowhere).

WordPress Foundations is our first publication. The purpose behind it was to provide a solid, up to date, foundational level knowledge of the WordPress platform, as well as giving you some tips and ideas on blogging as a medium.

With this book out of the way, more content will be coming out soon to help you in your newfound business.

We will be covering the various ways to get massive amounts of traffic to your website, leveraging the hottest technologies on the web.

We will be covering tools you can use to make small changes that make big impacts on your website.

WordPress Foundations The Course

WordPress Foundations the course takes what is taught here, and goes a lot more in depth. I wanted to keep this book focused on getting your site up and running, as quickly, and easily as possible.

If you buy this book from Amazon, I will offer you a **special discount** to upgrade to the course. WordPressFoundations.com is the site, after you checkout the site, and see if it is for you, type in:

www.wordpressfoundations.com/amazon

When you do this, you will get the course for a cheaper price. The difference between the two is the Amazon link will not include the book, so you still need this printed book. (The course **assumes** you have the book, and you do need it to complete the course, as I do not repeat most of the stuff covered in the book).

The course has several components.

You get a **quick start study guide**. This is based on the structure of how I would go about talking with you in real life. I would ask you questions, and have you make decisions based on the answer.

Each chapter has its own set of "**Action Steps**" that you can take that will REALLY get you ahead of the game. If you have no clue what your blog is about, you really should be checking out the videos.

You also get the **Videos**, of me going through a lot of this information, telling you what each chapter is about prior to reading it, things to look out for, and what you should do to get the MOST out of each chapter. You also get this in **AudioBook** format.

You will get to see videos of me going over different sections of WordPress, covering many of the topics covered here, but in **video format with me teaching you** while I got over the different interface options in real time. This should increase your ability to move around 10x.

My favorite part about the course is, I go over some more **advanced techniques**, and things that you REALLY need to know and get handled. (In both **video, and written worksheets**)

I cover **advanced content creation strategies**, showing you how to come up with ideas for your blog, how to structure them, and exploit them to your advantage so you will never be stuck trying to "think up something to say" again.

One of my favorite parts of the course is SEO (**Search Engine Optimization**). I teach you how to install a SEO plug-in, and take full advantage of it. SEO is a very advanced concept. If you hired a "real" SEO off elance.com or a firm, meaning someone who does it professionally (not some guy who read a book), it will typically run you about $1,500 for that person to look at your site, write down some suggestions, and send you the bill. I will be covering what that would typically cover in this course. I will also show you HOW to change these things. (Which could cost you so much more)

This is not going to be super in-depth, you do not NEED to know everything, but what I do cover, you REALLY need to know. It will be similar to this course. I will teach you what you need to know, without boring you to tears with technical mumbo jumbo (and trust me, SEO is FILLED with technical mumbo jumbo).

Your Free Bonuses

Do not forget to visit *EnlightenedWebmastery.com* and sign up for our newsletter, so you can get a free 15-20-page report on manipulating graphics online, as well as updates to this book.

If you would like to see something covered in more detail, do not be afraid to ask, I am very interested in your feedback. Contact me.

NOTES

Write down your account information, usernames, passwords, emails, URLs, for your hosting providers, blog, databases, etc. As well as the name of your site for reference.

If you do not wish to write it here, please write it on a 3.5-inch card and keep it with you, so you can keep track later on should you need to change something.

Made in the USA